EVERY *girl* HAS A *story*

THIS STORY BELONGS TO:

_____

GIRLHOOD

THE STORY

WHAT'S YOUR STORY?

EVERY GIRL HAS ONE.

It is the story of growing from a kid into a teenager and finally into an adult. The story of being a girl (girlhood) and growing into a young woman (womanhood).

You might find that you are growing up faster than your siblings or your friends. You might find that your siblings or friends are growing up faster than you. We want you to know that everyone's story of growing up is unique and should be celebrated.

However quickly or slowly you feel you may be growing, we want you to:

- ○ Remember that you are still you
- ○ Feel informed about what to expect and when
- ○ Know where or who to turn to if you have any questions

Most of all, however, we want you to celebrate every day of growing up; your unique experience, your unique journey, your story.

WHO IS THIS FOR?

Girlhood: The Story is part journal, part guide. It has been specifically designed for you, and other young girls who are entering puberty. We know your journey into womanhood can be exciting, but we also know that you might have a lot of questions about what is happening to your body and about how you're feeling.

That's why we have created this journal, to help you feel more informed. This is a space for you to write down your thoughts and track any patterns and changes that happen as you grow up.

You can also use Girlhood: The Story to help with any questions or conversations you have with your friends, family members or guardians.

'WE WANT THIS TO BECOME YOUR STORY, AS EVERY STORY IS UNIQUE. WE HOPE THIS WILL BECOME THE PERFECT COMPANION FOR YOU ON YOUR JOURNEY.'

Team Hood x

HOW TO USE

☼ ADVICE

Find out more about what changes you can expect, when you might experience them, where or who to turn to if you have any questions.

☼ GET CREATIVE

Make it your own by colouring in any or all of the illustrations on the different pages of your story. You can even create your own colour code to reflect each of your moods.

☼ CHAPTERS

Create a new chapter of your story every month. There are 12 chapters in here (enough for 1 year) so you can start your story whenever you are ready. For example, Chapter 1 can start in January or in March or in June. This is your story. It's up to you!

EACH CHAPTER INCLUDES...

☼ DAYS OF THE WEEK

Just like with a diary, you can make plans or write down what you did during the day.

☼ MYTHS AND TIPS

So you can find out more about what's true about growing up and what's not.

☼ A MOOD TRACKER

A quick way of noting how you are feeling on a particular day using your own colour code. You may find it helpful to keep track of how you are feeling and how it relates to your monthly cycle. It's not just about tracking pre-menstrual syndrome (PMS). Hormonal changes throughout the month and charting your emotions will help you to keep on top of your moods as they change.

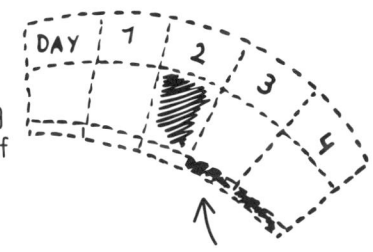

YOU CAN ALSO
LOG YOUR PERIOD
HERE TOO

'I've tracked my cycle for years. I find it super helpful to do so. It allows me to record my dates, duration, intensity and even how I've been feeling during each cycle.'

— JAZ RABADIA MBE

☼ A PERIOD TRACKER

Your period can be a good indicator of your overall health. By tracking and logging details of your cycle (such as blood flow, frequency and length), you will start to notice patterns and get to know your body that much better.

	JAN	FEB	MAR	APR	MAY
1	○	○	◑	◉	○
2	⊗	○	●	◉	⊗
3	⊗	○	●	⊘	○
4	◉	⊛	◐	◐	○

'Mark them in your calendar a couple of months in advance (using a period tracker app can help you predict when your next one will be). This will help you to adequately prepare for your period and welcome it into your life at that time rather than it just showing up and catching you off guard.'

— BAMI KUTEYI

YOUR BODY

As you grow older, you'll notice that your body may start to change and become more like an adult. This process is called puberty.

Changes can start at any time from 8 years of age to 13 years. It all begins when your brain sends off signals to certain parts of the body, telling them to start growing and changing. These signals are called hormones and they act as messengers in your body.

☼ SO WHAT ACTUALLY CHANGES IN PUBERTY?

During puberty, hormones can cause the following changes:

- You can grow taller and gain weight
- Your hips may get wider
- Your breasts start to grow
- You grow hair under your arms and around the vulva
- Your body odour may change
- You may get acne or pimples
- You get your first menstrual period

☼ WHAT IS A PERIOD?

A period (also known as menstruation) is monthly bleeding. It happens due to changes in the amount of hormones in your body.

Your period is part of something called your 'menstrual cycle'. The day you start your period is the first day of your menstrual cycle. The length of your menstrual cycle is the time from the start of one period to the start of the next one.

The changes you will experience throughout your menstrual cycle are the result of your body's hormones. The main ones to be aware of are oestrogen, progesterone, follicle-stimulating hormones and testosterone.

These hormones send signals to the ovaries inside your body to get them to release an egg. Once an egg has been released from an ovary, it moves into one of your fallopian tubes. At the same time, the lining of your uterus begins to grow and thicken. If the egg is not fertilised by sperm, pregnancy does not occur. The lining of your uterus then breaks down and flows out of the body through the vagina as blood. This is called menstruation, the menstrual period, or just your 'period'.

It usually takes about a month for the lining to build up, then break down. That is why most people get their periods around once a month. Your periods may not be regular at first and may vary in length until your body settles into its own natural rhythm. The typical length of your cycle is determined by your age, genes, health, body mass index (BMI) and other factors such as diet, stress and hormonal birth control.

☼ FEMALE REPRODUCTIVE SYSTEM

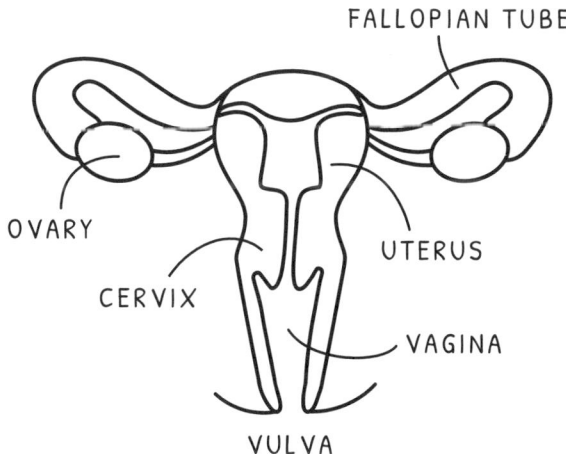

☼ WHEN DOES YOUR PERIOD START?

Periods usually start at any time between the ages of 8 and 18. It is important to remember that everyone is different and that people might experience their first periods at completely different ages from their friends, siblings or mums.

☼ HOW LONG DOES A PERIOD LAST FOR?

Each period usually lasts for 1 to 8 days but could last up to 10 days.

☼ HOW OFTEN WILL I GET MY PERIOD?

When you first start your periods, it is common for them to be a bit heavier. It takes a bit of time for your body to get used to the changes in your hormones. This means your periods might be irregular when you first start having them. Once your body has got into a routine, periods normally happen every 24 - 38 days.

☼ HOW WILL I KNOW THAT I HAVE GOT MY PERIOD?

You'll most likely see a reddish-brown mark on your pants or on your bed sheets when you wake up in the morning.

☼ WHAT IS CONSIDERED NORMAL FOR A PERIOD?

Since everyone is different, the amount of blood they lose with each period can be different too. The majority of blood loss occurs during the first 2 days and some people experience menstrual (abdominal) cramps, back and leg ache too.

When your period is at its heaviest, the blood will be red. On lighter days, it may be pink, brown or black. You can use specially designed period products to absorb or collect blood loss during your period.

It is important to change or clean the period products you use to absorb or collect the blood loss regularly. This will keep you feeling and smelling fresh and will help prevent blood from marking your clothes or your bedding. Have a look at the Period Products section of this journal for more details.

☼ WHAT IF MY PERIODS ARE HEAVY?

If your periods are very heavy, blood might soak through your period products onto your clothes or your bedding. Another sign of really heavy bleeding is that you might notice large blood clots (bigger than 1cm) in the blood you lose during your period.

If you think your periods are unusually heavy, you can talk to your GP who will be able to recommend any treatment you may need to make your periods easier to manage.

☼ WHEN DO PERIODS STOP?

Periods are usually experienced until you are in your late 40s to mid-50s.

☼ HOW CAN I PREPARE FOR MY PERIOD?

It's best to be prepared for your periods, even if yours have not started yet. Tracking your moods and how your body feels can help. Have pads, tampons or a menstrual cup ready at home or carry some with you to school. This way you can be sure you have them if you need them.

☼ WHAT ELSE DO I NEED TO KNOW?

Periods are a natural, healthy part of any girl's life. You can carry on having fun, being active and enjoying life. What really matters is that your periods shouldn't stop you from doing anything that you want to do. If they are affecting negatively - for example, stopping you from going to school because they are painful or heavy, talk to your GP who will be able to help.

PERIOD PRODUCTS

There are two main types of period products you can choose to use - those that are external (like pads and period pants), and those that are internal (like tampons and menstrual cups). There is a good range of products to choose from and to experiment with to find out what works best for you. You can either choose to stick with one product or switch between products depending on what works best for you at the time.

Have a read below to find out more about what you can choose to use:

☼ TAMPONS

Many girls choose to use tampons as they find them more convenient, especially when playing sports or going swimming. A tampon is a small, single-use cotton plug that you can insert into your vagina to absorb your flow. Tampons come with applicators to help with insertion and a cord to help with removal. It can take some practice to get the hang of, so give it a couple of tries. Remember to change your tampons regularly (at least every 4-8 hours), ensure your hands are clean when handling and inserting tampons and use a tampon that has the lowest absorbency that is suitable for your period flow. Following these tips can help reduce the risk of Toxic Shock Syndrome (a rare but life-threatening condition that can be caused by bacteria getting into your body).

☼ PADS

Most girls use a pad when they first get their period. Single-use pads are made of cotton and have sticky strips that attach to your underwear. You can also use reusable pads that are available in organic cotton or

bamboo cloth. These are more environmentally sustainable as they can be used multiple times. Be sure to wash them regularly so they are always ready for your next use. Both single-use and reusable pads come in all shapes and sizes so you can pick one that suits you and your flow.

MENSTRUAL CUPS

Menstrual cups are another popular choice. They are reusable and each one can last up to 10 years so they are considered to be environmentally sustainable. It is a flexible silicone cup that can be folded up and inserted inside your vagina. The cup will collect your menstrual blood and needs to be emptied every 4-6 hours, depending on your flow. Always make sure your cup is cleaned thoroughly after each use. The cups come in all sorts of sizes and shapes so you can find one that works just right for you.

PERIOD PANTS

Period pants are the newest kid on the block! They have been recently created to make your periods even more comfortable. They look and act like normal underwear and, on the plus side, also absorb your menstrual blood without any leaks or any need for other period products. They have anti-odour and anti-microbial properties so they stay fresh and you don't have to worry about odours or staining your usual underwear.

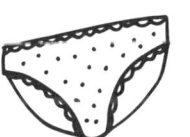

PERIOD APPS

Want to up your period tracking game? If you have a smartphone or tablet, period apps are a great way to track your periods and get useful reminders and insights specific to your cycle. There are lots of apps to choose from - available on Android or iOS app stores.

THE PERIOD MUNCHIES

What we eat plays such an important role in our health, our moods, our energy levels and our hormones. Often, period hormones can make us feel like we have a galaxy of emotions swirling around, making us sometimes feel irritable, teary, low in energy and uncomfortable.

This is all normal. The great thing is, by eating the right foods you can limit how these hormones affect your feelings.

We're always told to eat our greens and veggies but sometimes eating this food might not seem as appealing as a takeaway or a bar of your favourite chocolate. The food we eat is information for every cell in our body and eating the right food can really help you to keep being your best self and lessen those period symptoms.

The problem with take away food and processed food like cakes, chocolate bars, pizzas and biscuits is that they're often high in sugar, salt and bad fats, and they contain little or no nutrients. The period is the time of the month when we most need healthy food containing vitamins and minerals like iron, vitamin B12 and folic acid that help our bodies create more red blood cells during our period. Eating too much sugar is especially bad for us during this time as it disrupts our hormones even more and can make those gnarly symptoms feel worse by causing low moods, sugar slumps and anxious feelings. Sugar can also affect the absorption of vitamins and minerals.

We often think of healthy food as being boring and a bit of a punishment, especially when we're

eat-&-feel GOOD

craving a big bowl of ice cream or a doughnut. The reason we crave sugar during our period is that our feel-good hormone serotonin dips and the stress hormone cortisol rises, which can affect our blood sugar levels. In an attempt to balance this, our extraordinary bodies try to find quick sources of energy. The good news is there are lots of delicious and nutritious foods you can eat to beat sugar cravings while still nourishing your growing, changing body and providing it with the nutrients it needs.

When it comes to healthy food it doesn't have to be a big bowl of sprouts. There are lots of healthy recipes that are packed with goodness and taste better than the shop-bought versions.

When you eat real 'whole food' ingredients they're easier for your body to digest and use for energy. They keep your blood sugars steady and supply you with all the nutrients your body needs leading up to and during your period. The next time you get hit with a big sugar craving, you could try making my homemade sugar-free brownies, bounties, snickers or chocolate nice-cream. They are made using healthy, simple ingredients packed with vitamins, fibre and much-needed minerals that will boost energy, help moods, improve skin, give you more focus and improve sleep.

These treats will keep you feeling full, fabulous and like the superstar you are!

LEISA COCKAYNE
INSTAGRAM: @makemesugarfre

Period
TRACKER

- ⊖ MUNCHIES
- ⊗ HEADACHE
- ⊛ ACNE
- ⊙ CRAMPS
- ⊘ TIRED

MY PERIOD

ADD A COLOUR CODE:

- ◇ LIGHT
- ◈ MEDIUM
- ◈ HEAVY

	JANUARY	FEBRUARY	MARCH	APRIL	MAY	JUNE	JULY	AUGUST	SEPTEMBER	OCTOBER	NOVEMBER	DECEMBER
1	○	○	○	○	○	○	○	○	○	○	○	○
2	○	○	○	○	○	○	○	○	○	○	○	○
3	○	○	○	○	○	○	○	○	○	○	○	○
4	○	○	○	○	○	○	○	○	○	○	○	○
5	○	○	○	○	○	○	○	○	○	○	○	○
6	○	○	○	○	○	○	○	○	○	○	○	○
7	○	○	○	○	○	○	○	○	○	○	○	○
8	○	○	○	○	○	○	○	○	○	○	○	○
9	○	○	○	○	○	○	○	○	○	○	○	○
10	○	○	○	○	○	○	○	○	○	○	○	○
11	○	○	○	○	○	○	○	○	○	○	○	○
12	○	○	○	○	○	○	○	○	○	○	○	○
13	○	○	○	○	○	○	○	○	○	○	○	○
14	○	○	○	○	○	○	○	○	○	○	○	○
15	○	○	○	○	○	○	○	○	○	○	○	○
16	○	○	○	○	○	○	○	○	○	○	○	○
17	○	○	○	○	○	○	○	○	○	○	○	○
18	○	○	○	○	○	○	○	○	○	○	○	○
19	○	○	○	○	○	○	○	○	○	○	○	○
20	○	○	○	○	○	○	○	○	○	○	○	○
21	○	○	○	○	○	○	○	○	○	○	○	○
22	○	○	○	○	○	○	○	○	○	○	○	○
23	○	○	○	○	○	○	○	○	○	○	○	○
24	○	○	○	○	○	○	○	○	○	○	○	○
25	○	○	○	○	○	○	○	○	○	○	○	○
26	○	○	○	○	○	○	○	○	○	○	○	○
27	○	○	○	○	○	○	○	○	○	○	○	○
28	○	○	○	○	○	○	○	○	○	○	○	○
29	○	○	○	○	○	○	○	○	○	○	○	○
30	○	○	○	○	○	○	○	○	○	○	○	○
31	○	○	○	○	○	○	○	○	○	○	○	○

PERIOD TRACKING NOTES

TRACK YOUR FLOW

JANUARY

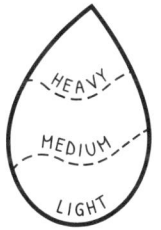

HEAVY

MEDIUM

LIGHT

FEBRUARY

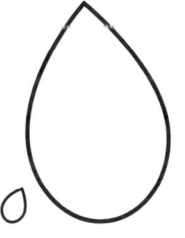

MARCH

APRIL

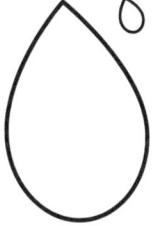

PERIOD TRACKING NOTES

MAY

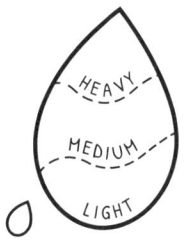

HEAVY

MEDIUM

LIGHT

JUNE

JULY

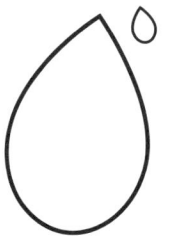

AUGUST

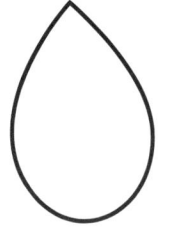

 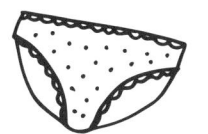

HOW ARE YOU FEELING?

SEPTEMBER

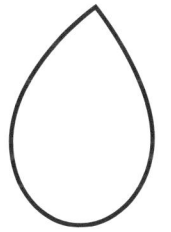

OCTOBER

NOVEMBER

DECEMBER

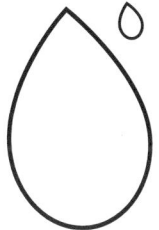

CHAPTER ONE

GRL PWR

I was absolutely desperate to start my period, as it was all anyone talked about at school. On a Friday night at home, after our family meal, I had three Creme Eggs - as you do - and then got a really bad tummy ache. My Mum said it was my fault as, apparently, it's not a good idea to eat three Creme Eggs at once... But I knew it was a different type of pain. I went to bed and when I woke up in the morning, there was a small brown stain in my knickers. I was absolutely delighted! My mum gave me a pantyliner, but my older sister said that wasn't big enough and sorted me out with a pad. But my mum did proudly tell the whole family, which I was majorly embarrassed by, even though I was excited to tell everyone at school.

GABBY EDLIN
CEO AND FOUNDER,
BLOODY GOOD PERIOD

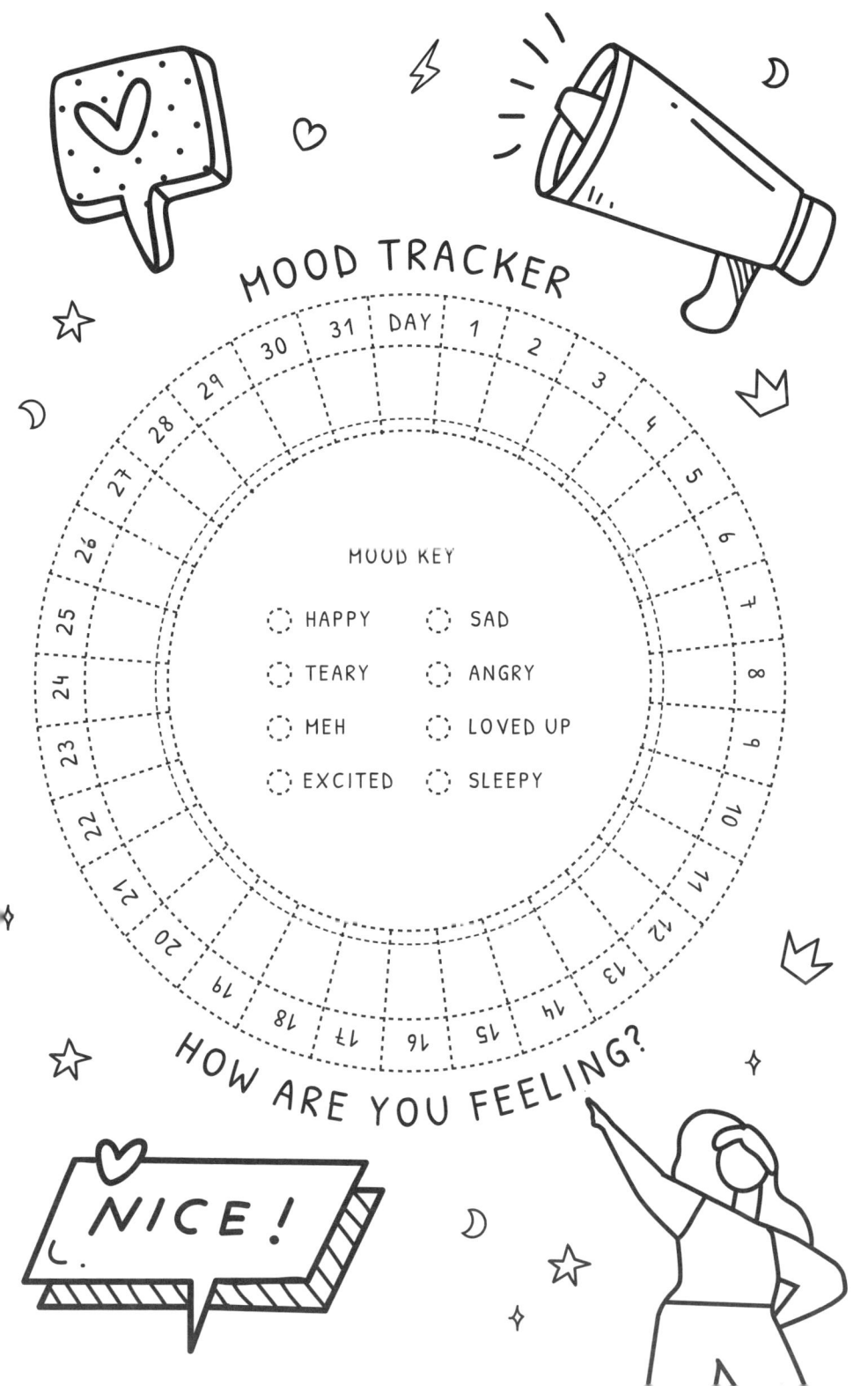

CHAPTER ONE

!AWESOME ♡

MONDAY

TUESDAY

WEDNESDAY

THURSDAY

FRIDAY

MYTH

PERIODS WILL LAST 7 DAYS

Periods can last anything from 1 - 8 days. How long they last can be different for everyone. Periods can be irregular, especially when they first begin, so no need to worry, just use the period tracker to see what your cycle is like.

SATURDAY

SUNDAY

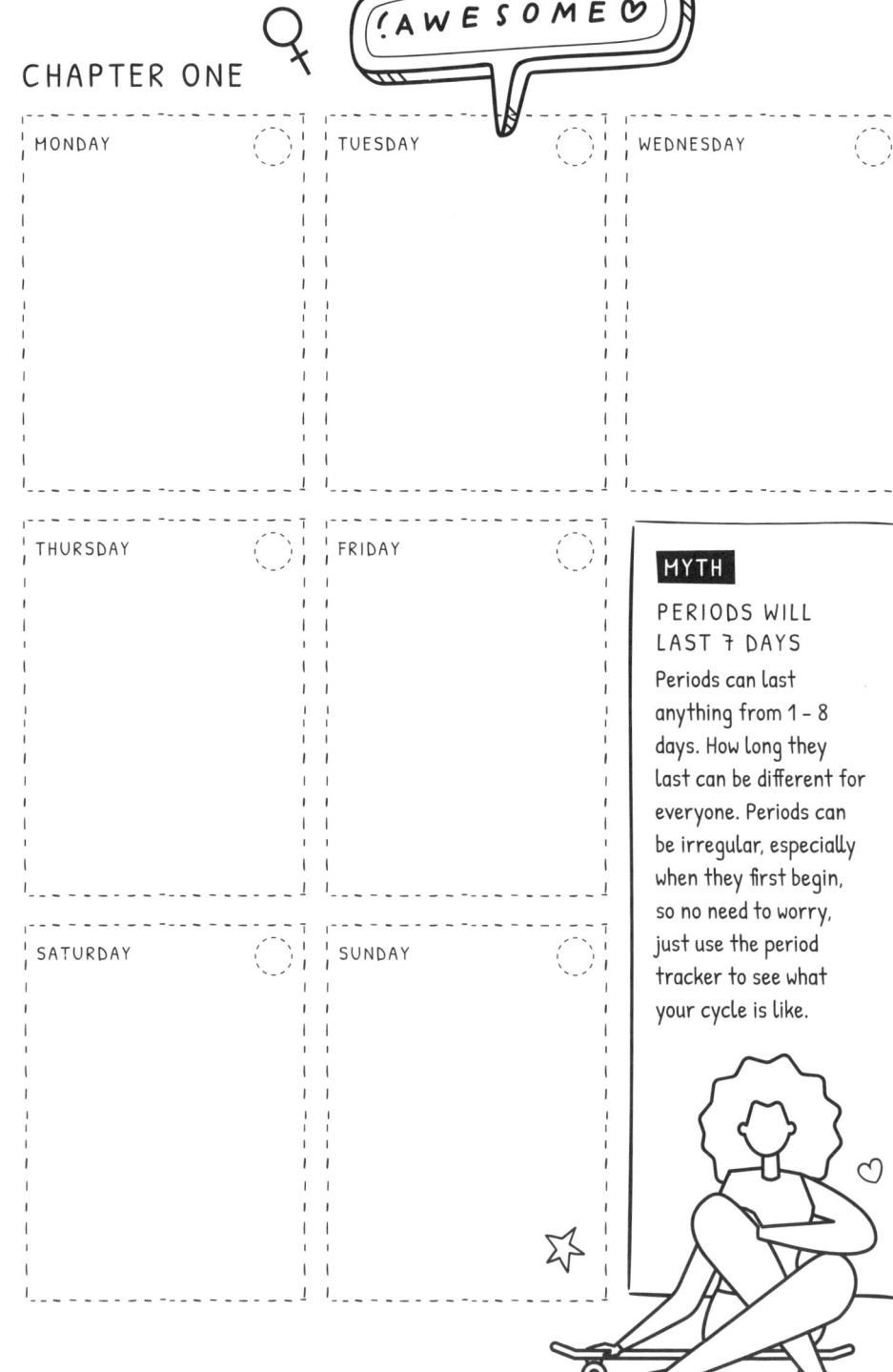

HOW'S YOUR WEEK GOING?

MONDAY	TUESDAY	WEDNESDAY

THURSDAY	FRIDAY	SATURDAY

SUNDAY	THINGS TO REMEMBER

CHAPTER ONE

MONDAY	TUESDAY	WEDNESDAY

THURSDAY	FRIDAY	NOTES

SATURDAY	SUNDAY	

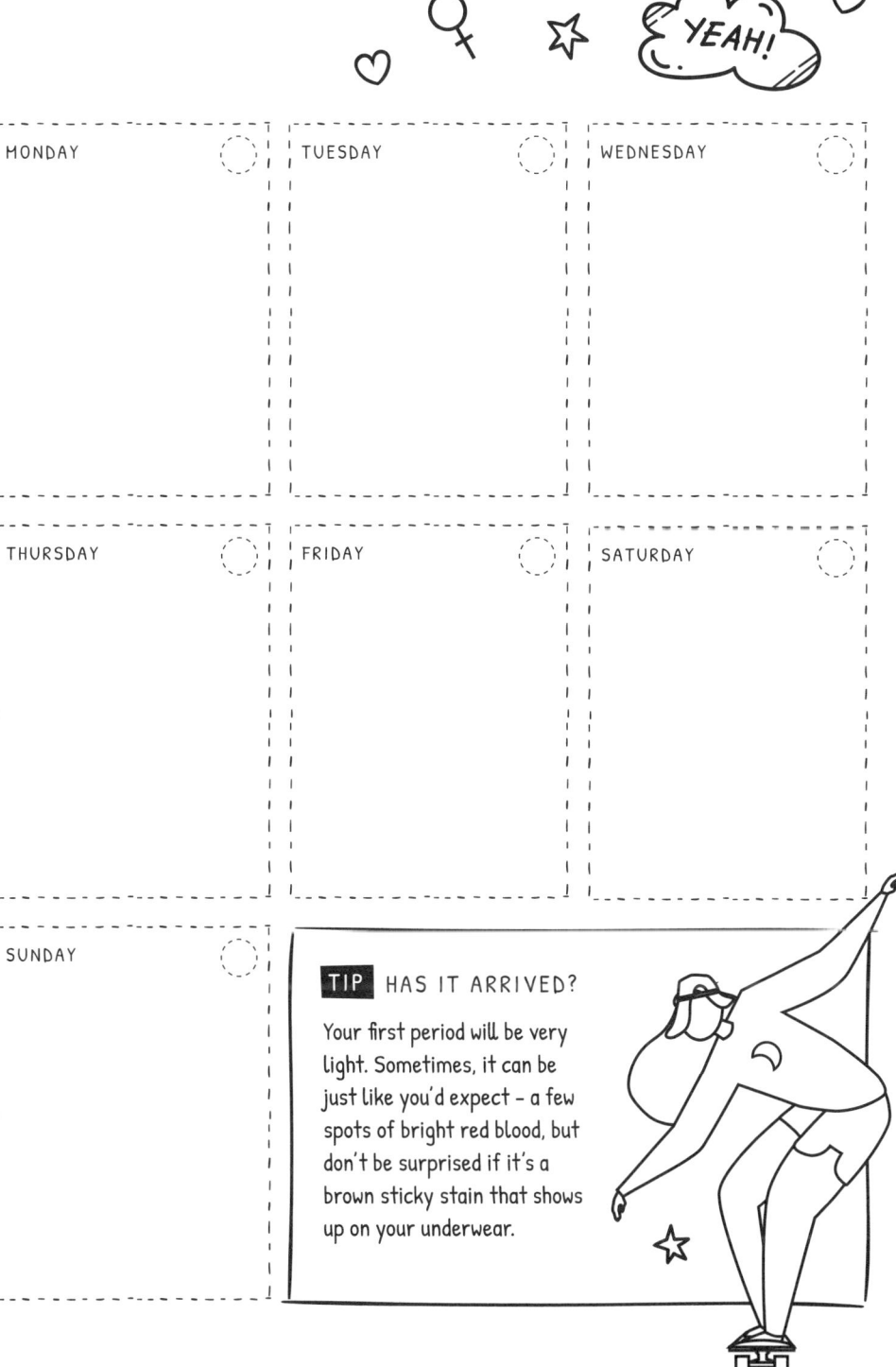

MONDAY

TUESDAY

WEDNESDAY

THURSDAY

FRIDAY

SATURDAY

SUNDAY

TIP HAS IT ARRIVED?

Your first period will be very light. Sometimes, it can be just like you'd expect - a few spots of bright red blood, but don't be surprised if it's a brown sticky stain that shows up on your underwear.

YEAH!

CHAPTER ONE ♡ ☽

MONDAY ○	TUESDAY ○	WEDNESDAY ○

THURSDAY ○	FRIDAY ○	NOTES

SATURDAY ○	SUNDAY ○	

♡

TO DO

○

○

○

○

○

○

○

○

○

○

○

○

○

○

COOL!

'We realise the importance of our voices only when we are silenced.'

— MALALA YOUSAFZAI

CHAPTER
two

It wasn't until I was 16 that my period finally arrived. I remember feeling left out or thinking something was wrong with me as all my friends had their first years before me. But I spoke to my mum about it and she explained she started hers at 16 too. My first period happened whilst I was riding my bike (home, thankfully), I noticed feeling a sudden urge to go to the loo and as I did I wiped away red. I didn't panic. Although I was a little scared, I mostly felt relieved. I grabbed the free pads we'd been given at school (that I'd been keeping safely tucked away at the back of my cupboard for 3 years) and proudly put my first one to use! Finally!

JAZ RABADIA MBE
ENERGY, SUSTAINABILITY & SOCIAL
IMPACT DIRECTOR

$E = mc^2$

$\sqrt{xy}$

$\alpha =$

θ

$F = m.a$

(x,y)

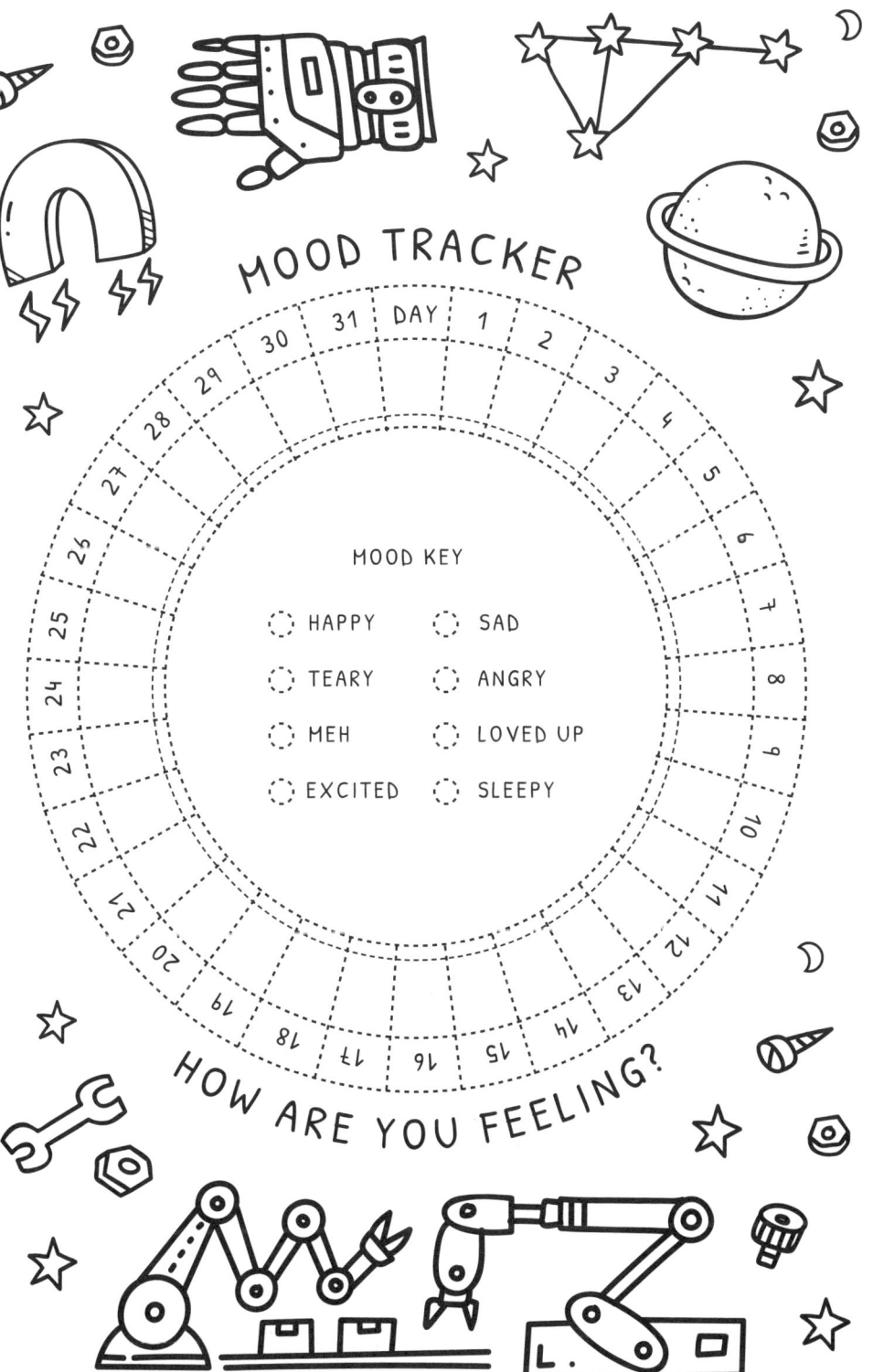

CHAPTER TWO

MONDAY

TUESDAY

WEDNESDAY

THURSDAY

FRIDAY

MYTH

MENSTRUAL CYCLES ARE 28 DAYS LONG AND WILL ALWAYS START ON TIME

How long you have to wait for your next period can be an average of 28 days, but remember everyone is different and your body will settle into its own natural rhythm.

SATURDAY

SUNDAY

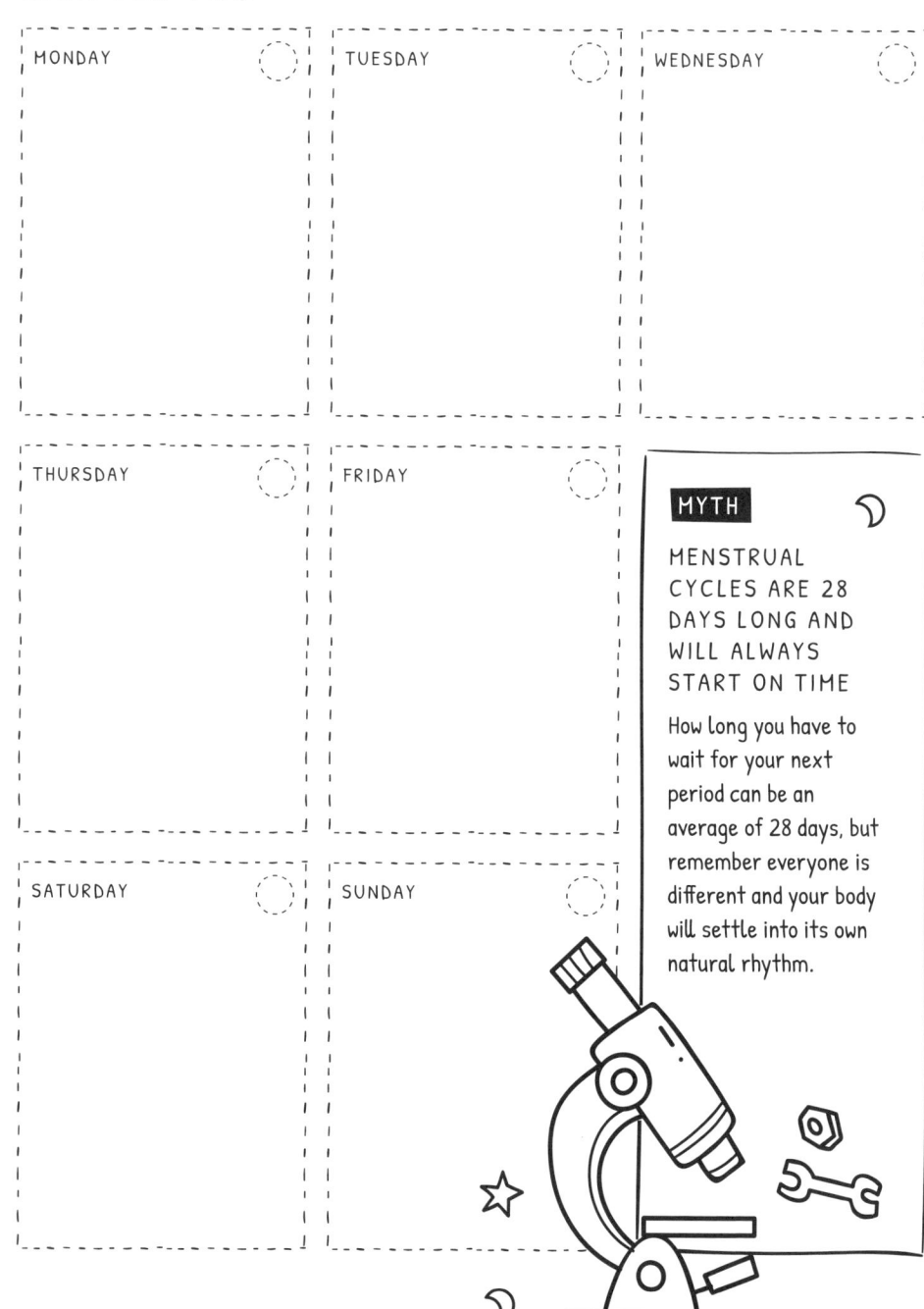

HOW'S YOUR WEEK GOING?

MONDAY

TUESDAY

WEDNESDAY

THURSDAY

FRIDAY

SATURDAY

SUNDAY

THINGS TO REMEMBER

DESIGN

CHAPTER TWO

MONDAY	TUESDAY	WEDNESDAY

THURSDAY	FRIDAY	NOTES

SATURDAY	SUNDAY	

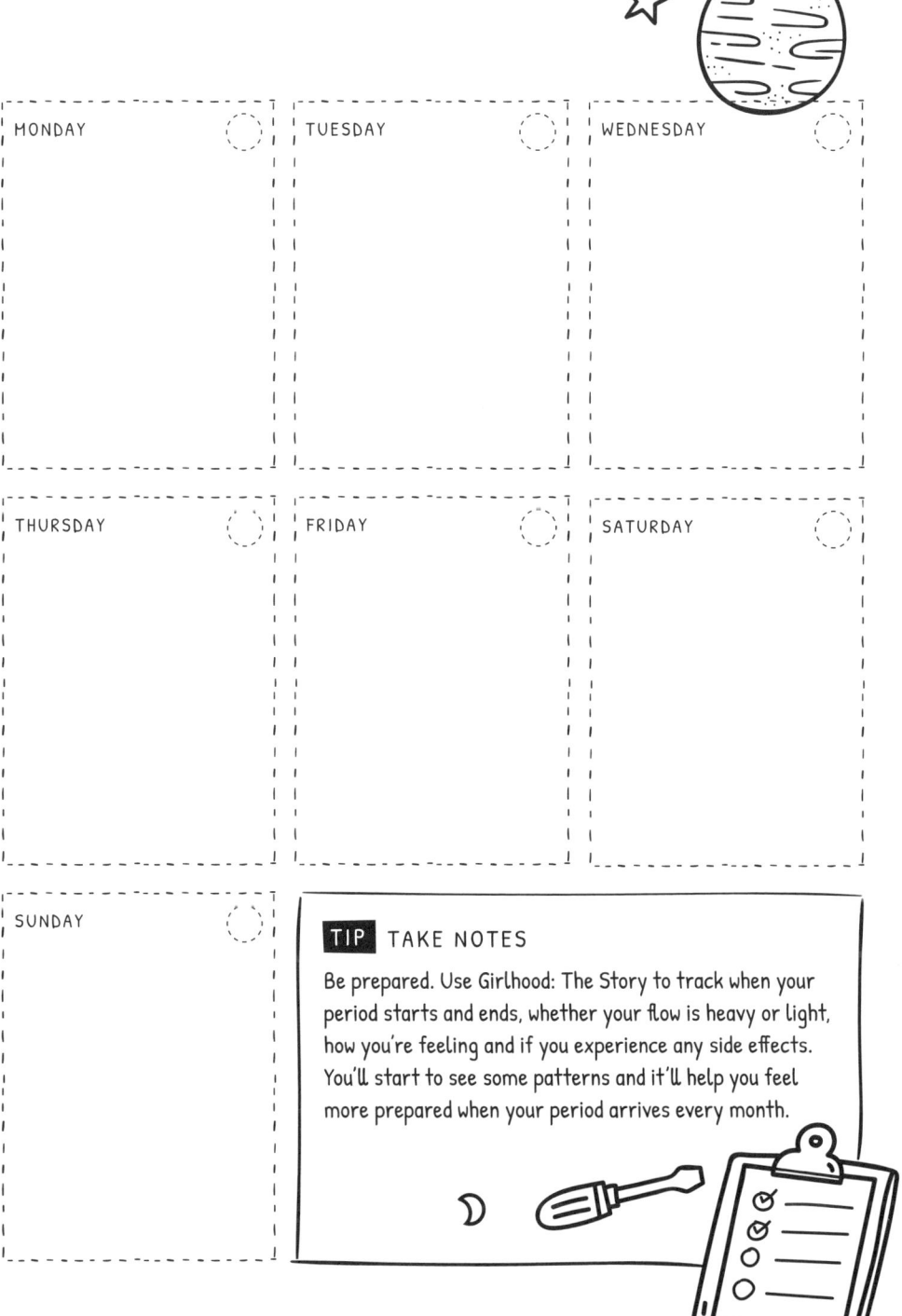

MONDAY

TUESDAY

WEDNESDAY

THURSDAY

FRIDAY

SATURDAY

SUNDAY

TIP TAKE NOTES

Be prepared. Use Girlhood: The Story to track when your period starts and ends, whether your flow is heavy or light, how you're feeling and if you experience any side effects. You'll start to see some patterns and it'll help you feel more prepared when your period arrives every month.

CHAPTER TWO

MONDAY

TUESDAY

WEDNESDAY

THURSDAY

FRIDAY

NOTES

SATURDAY

SUNDAY

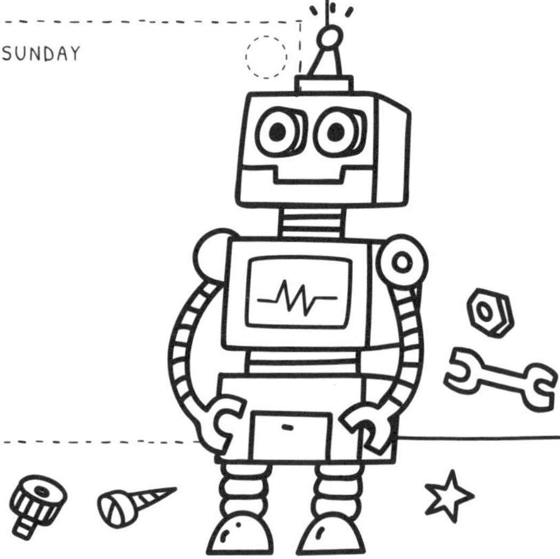

TO DO

◌

◌

◌

◌

◌

◌

◌

◌

◌

◌

◌

◌

◌

◌

'Being confident and believing in your own self-worth
is necessary to achieving your potential.'

— SHERYL SANDBERG

SPACE FOR DOODLES

TIP LEND A HELPING HAND

Remember, your friends may also be going through or expecting their first periods. Help out by offering them a pad or tampon if you think they need one. This helps breaks the awkwardness of talking about it. And remember, we have all had that experience of having a leak and getting blood on our jeans or skirt, so be discreet and kind, and try to help them out.

CHAPTER 3

I didn't start my period until I was 15 years old, I worried quite a bit that all my other friends had started and I was the last one! What if it never came? When friends talked about it I pretended that I had too. I remember worrying terribly that there was something wrong with me. It wasn't until I spoke to a classmate that I realised that I wasn't the only one, she too hadn't and she explained that her older sister had started late and that it was all very normal. Everyone's comes at different times! Starting late meant that I was fully aware of what to do but even so it came as a bit of a shock!

JO-JO ELLISON
HEAD OF FILM PRODUCTION & FILM
PRODUCER, ARCHER'S MARK

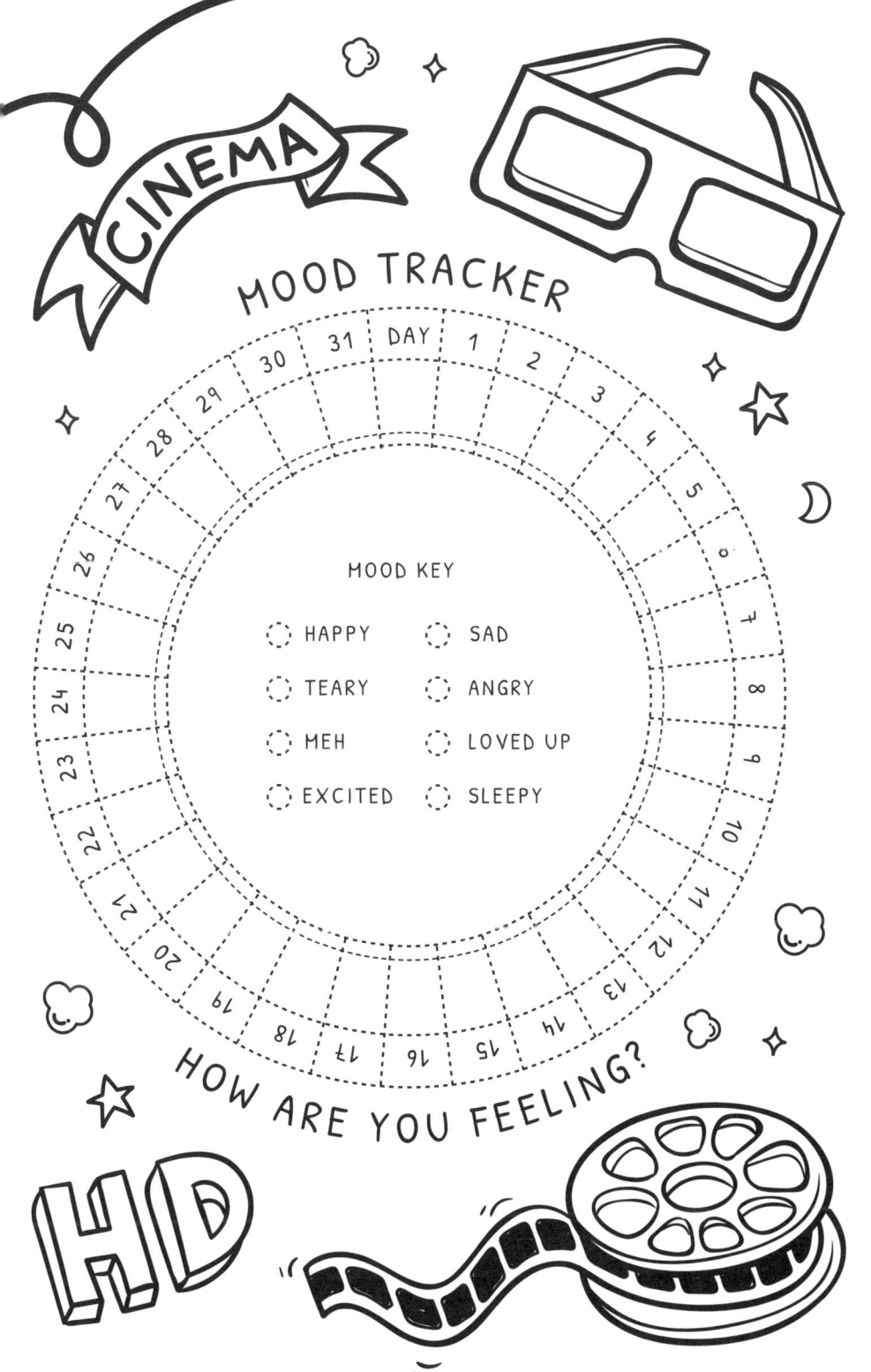

CINEMA

MOOD TRACKER

30 31 DAY 1 2 3 4 5 6 7 8 9 10 11 12 13 14 15 16 17 18 19 20 21 22 23 24 25 26 27 28 29

MOOD KEY

○ HAPPY   ○ SAD

○ TEARY   ○ ANGRY

○ MEH   ○ LOVED UP

○ EXCITED   ○ SLEEPY

HOW ARE YOU FEELING?

HD

CHAPTER THREE

MONDAY

TUESDAY

WEDNESDAY

THURSDAY

FRIDAY

MYTH

YOU SHOULDN'T USE A TAMPON UNTIL YOU'RE OLD ENOUGH

From your very first period you can choose whatever works best for you. Have a look at all the products available in the section on Period Products. Feel free to try tampons. Just read the instructions carefully and ask your mum or another trusted adult for guidance.

SATURDAY

SUNDAY

HOW'S YOUR WEEK GOING?

MONDAY	TUESDAY	WEDNESDAY

THURSDAY	FRIDAY	SATURDAY

SUNDAY	THINGS TO REMEMBER

CHAPTER THREE

MONDAY

TUESDAY

WEDNESDAY

THURSDAY

FRIDAY

NOTES

SATURDAY

SUNDAY

MONDAY	TUESDAY	WEDNESDAY

THURSDAY	FRIDAY	SATURDAY

SUNDAY

TIP CREATE A PERIOD PACK

Sometimes your period can come on when you're not near home. So you don't get caught out, create a period pack for yourself that you can pop into your bag or backpack. Just put a few essentials like extra underwear and a pad/tampon into a small zipped bag and you'll always be ready!

CHAPTER THREE

MONDAY	TUESDAY	WEDNESDAY

THURSDAY	FRIDAY	NOTES

SATURDAY	SUNDAY	

TO DO

○ -

○ -

○ -

○ -

○ -

○ -

○ -

○ -

○ -

○ -

○ -

○ -

○ -

○ -

'It takes a great deal of courage to stand up to your
enemies, but even more to stand up to your friends.'

— J. K. ROWLING

CHAPTER
four

I was 8 years old when I began my period. I remember being in year 4 in primary school, going to the toilets at break-time and seeing blood in my pants. I was so scared of what it was that I ignored it and went through another 4 hours of school as I didn't want to tell anybody. I was extremely scared, but when I got home my mum helped me and told me what was happening (that I had started my period!) and what to do. I treated it as normal, because it is normal!

MOLLY FENTON
FOUNDER, LOVE YOUR PERIOD CAMPAIGN

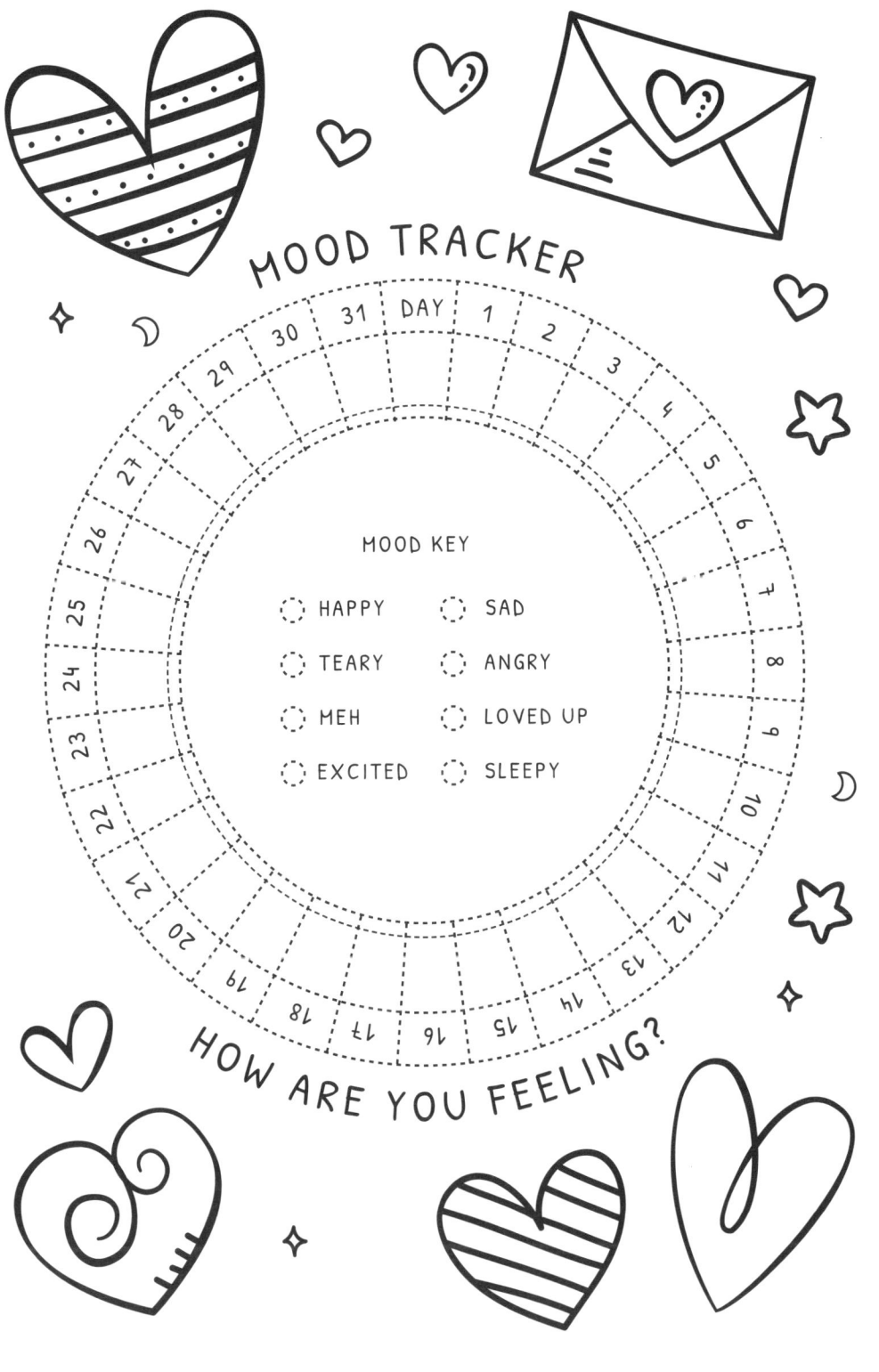

MOOD TRACKER

30 31 DAY 1 2 3 4 5 6 7 8 9 10 11 12 13 14 15 16 17 18 19 20 21 22 23 24 25 26 27 28 29

MOOD KEY

○ HAPPY   ○ SAD

○ TEARY   ○ ANGRY

○ MEH   ○ LOVED UP

○ EXCITED   ○ SLEEPY

HOW ARE YOU FEELING?

CHAPTER FOUR

| MONDAY ○ | TUESDAY ○ | WEDNESDAY ○ |

| THURSDAY ○ | FRIDAY ○ |

MYTH

A TAMPON CAN GET LOST INSIDE THE VAGINA

No need to worry as this is not true. The cervix opening at the top of your vagina is too small for the tampon to move into. If you feel your tampon does ride up, it has a handy string to help you pull it back out.

| SATURDAY ○ | SUNDAY ○ |

HOW'S YOUR WEEK GOING?

MONDAY

TUESDAY

WEDNESDAY

THURSDAY

FRIDAY

SATURDAY

SUNDAY

THINGS TO REMEMBER

CHAPTER FOUR

MONDAY	TUESDAY	WEDNESDAY

THURSDAY	FRIDAY	NOTES

SATURDAY	SUNDAY	

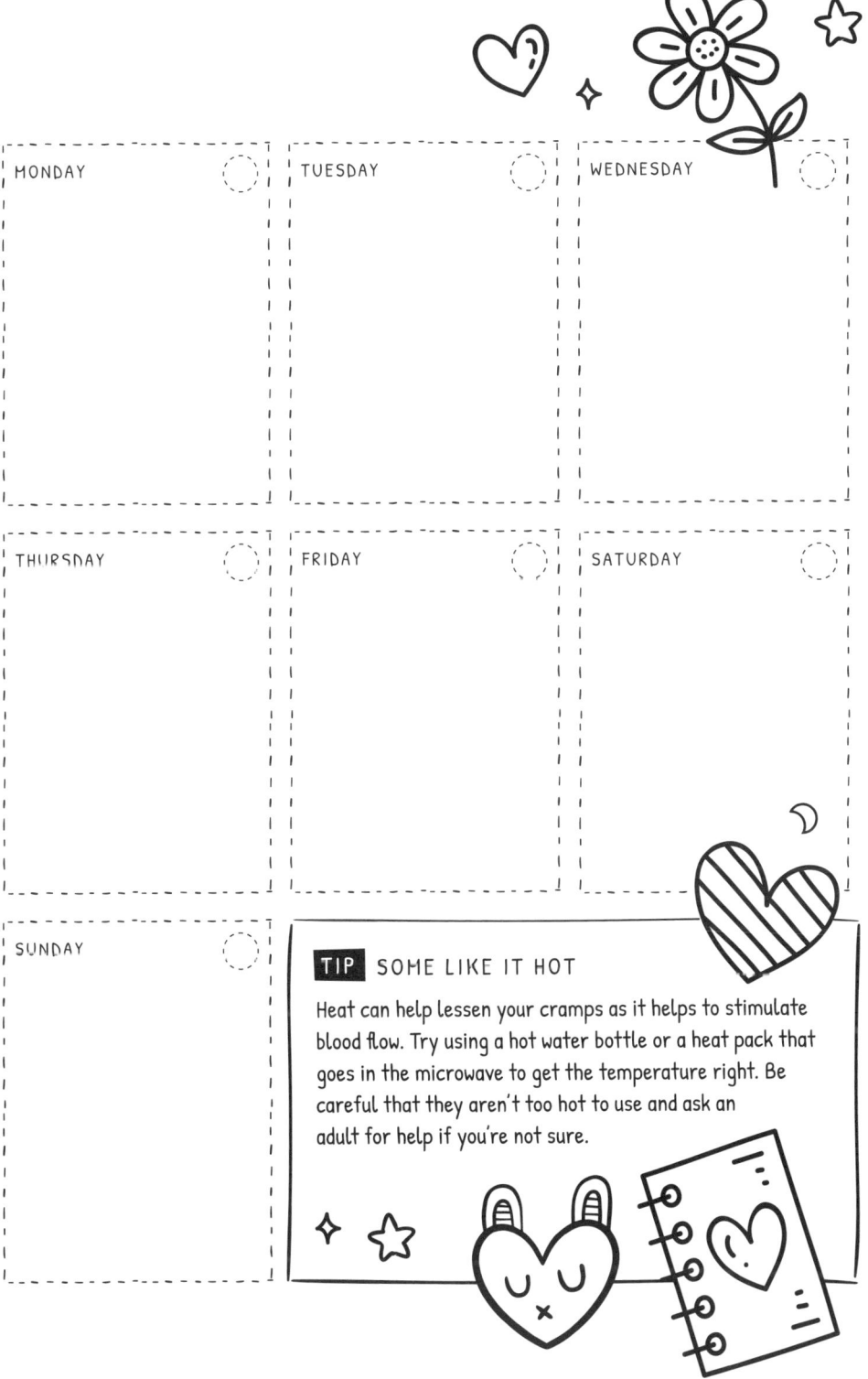

MONDAY

TUESDAY

WEDNESDAY

THURSDAY

FRIDAY

SATURDAY

SUNDAY

TIP SOME LIKE IT HOT

Heat can help lessen your cramps as it helps to stimulate blood flow. Try using a hot water bottle or a heat pack that goes in the microwave to get the temperature right. Be careful that they aren't too hot to use and ask an adult for help if you're not sure.

CHAPTER FOUR

MONDAY ○

TUESDAY ○

WEDNESDAY ○

THURSDAY ○

FRIDAY ○

NOTES ✦

SATURDAY ○

SUNDAY ○

TO DO

- ○ ----------------------------------
- ○ ----------------------------------
- ○ ----------------------------------
- ○ ----------------------------------
- ○ ----------------------------------
- ○ ----------------------------------
- ○ ----------------------------------

- ○ ----------------------------------
- ○ ----------------------------------
- ○ ----------------------------------
- ○ ----------------------------------
- ○ ----------------------------------
- ○ ----------------------------------
- ○ ----------------------------------

'Your story is what you have, what you will always have. It is something to own.'

— MICHELLE OBAMA

SPACE FOR
Photos

CHAPTER 5

I was 14 when I first had my period. I remember a lot of girls at school had started their periods, and I felt like I must have been one of the last girls in my year to even start mine!! I remember a lot of my friends complaining of sore stomachs and this left me in no rush for my own period to start!

I used to get the bus to and from school every day with my brother and we would race home to get changed and get outside and play with our friends. This day was no different. We raced home and got changed and I needed the loo before quickly following my brother outside. As he raced down the stairs to join the other kids outside I remember seeing a few red drops splash into the toilet which startled me at first. Soon my logical side kicked in and I realised I wasn't dying I had just started my period!

I felt quite happy that I had started it and as my mum was still at work I stupidly told my brother who went and told everyone outside! But I didn't care. My mum taught me young never to be ashamed of things like my period so I cracked on, went outside and played football with the boys till she came home.

SERENA MONIQUE GUTHRIE MBE
ENGLAND NETBALL 2019

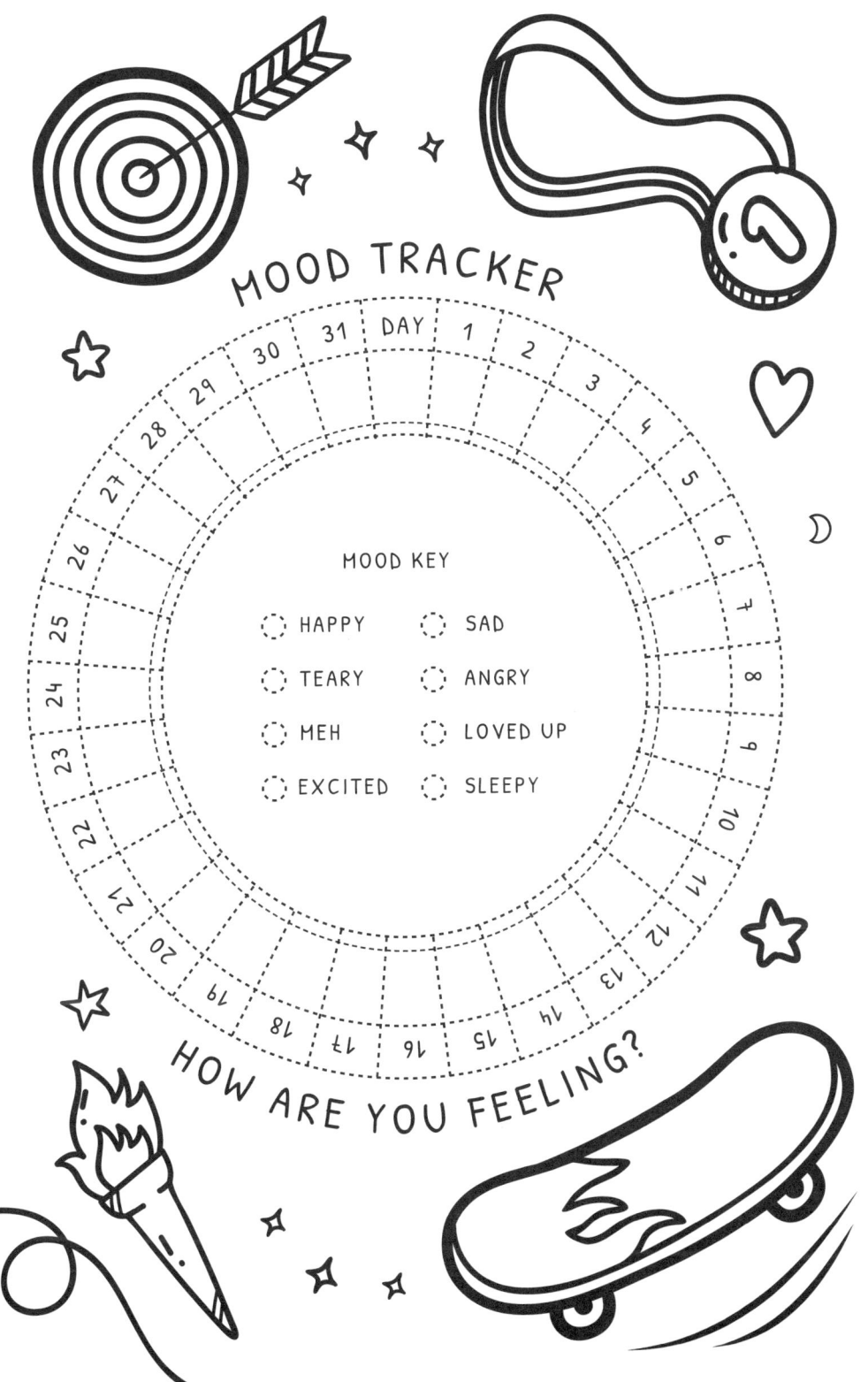

CHAPTER FIVE

MONDAY

TUESDAY

WEDNESDAY

THURSDAY

FRIDAY

YOU SHOULDN'T HAVE A BATH WHEN ON YOUR PERIOD AS HOT WATER INCREASES BLOOD FLOW

Some people think having a bath during your period is unsafe or will increase your blood flow. In actual fact, nothing other than your body can change your blood flow. So feel free to enjoy a nice warm bath or to use a hot water bottle, as you'll find this can help you to relax and ease cramps.

SATURDAY

SUNDAY

HOW'S YOUR WEEK GOING?

MONDAY

TUESDAY

WEDNESDAY

THURSDAY

FRIDAY

SATURDAY

SUNDAY

THINGS TO REMEMBER

CHAPTER FIVE

MONDAY

TUESDAY

WEDNESDAY

THURSDAY

FRIDAY

NOTES

SATURDAY

SUNDAY

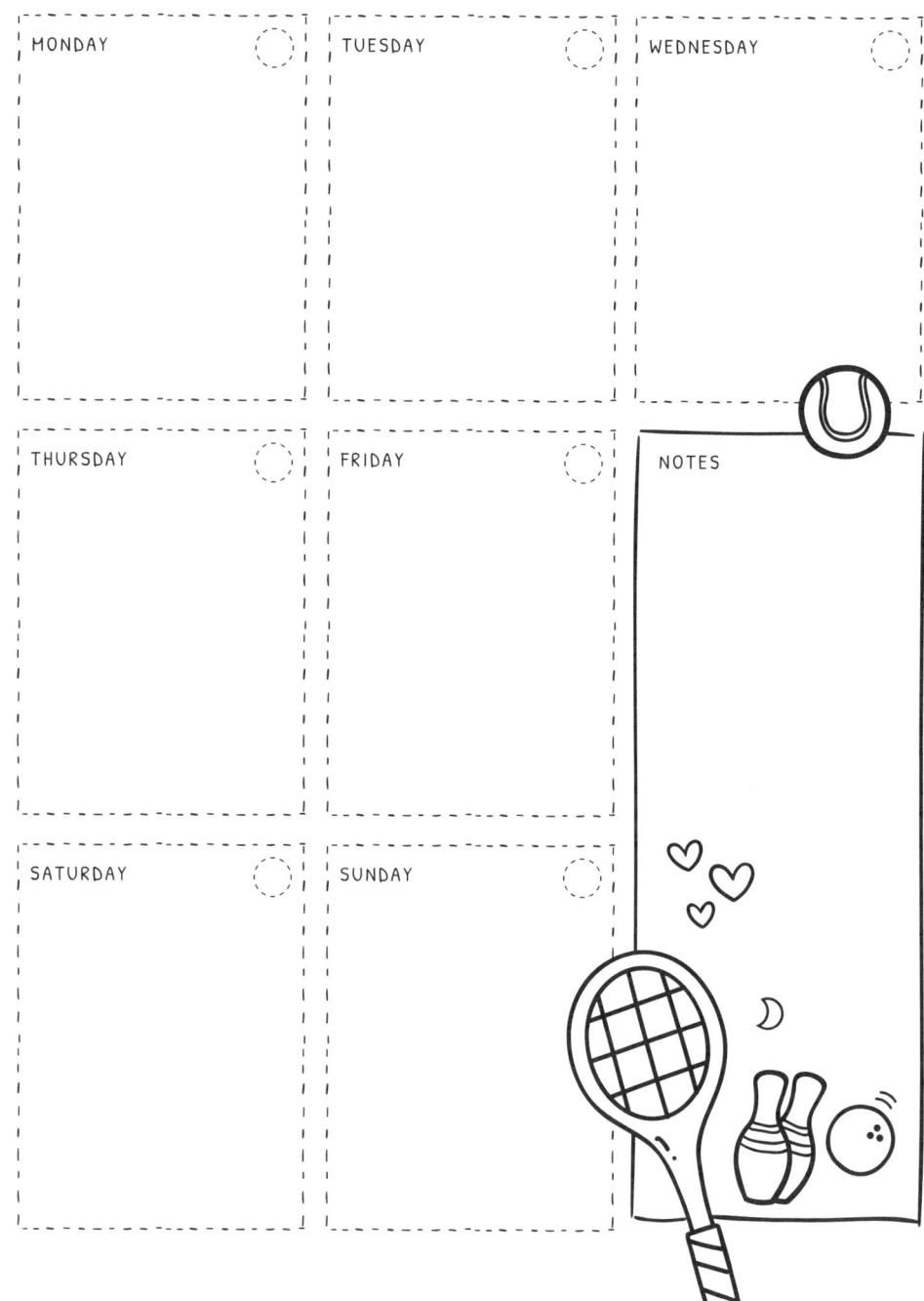

MONDAY	TUESDAY	WEDNESDAY

THURSDAY	FRIDAY	SATURDAY

SUNDAY

QUOTE OF THE WEEK

'Exercise really does help beat those cramps. My PE teacher would tell me this every time I would try and skip lessons at school, and even though I'd never admit she was right, I always felt much better after doing something energetic.'

— MATILDA STANLEY

CHAPTER FIVE

MONDAY	TUESDAY	WEDNESDAY

THURSDAY	FRIDAY	NOTES

SATURDAY	SUNDAY	

TO DO

○ --------------------------------   ○ --------------------------------

○ --------------------------------   ○ --------------------------------

○ --------------------------------   ○ --------------------------------

○ --------------------------------   ○ --------------------------------

○ --------------------------------   ○ --------------------------------

○ --------------------------------   ○ --------------------------------

○ --------------------------------   ○ --------------------------------

'Different is good.'

— SERENA WILLIAMS

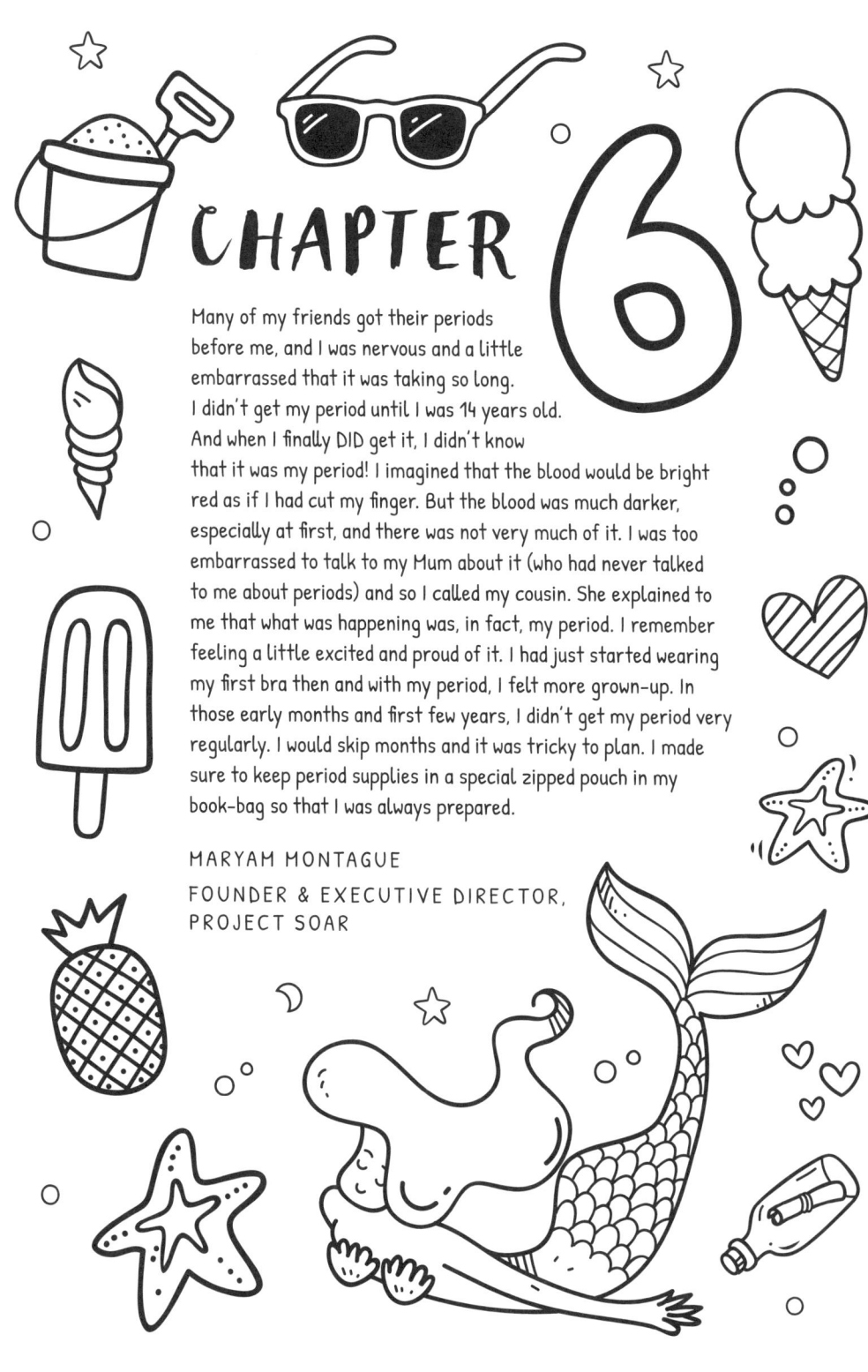

CHAPTER 6

Many of my friends got their periods before me, and I was nervous and a little embarrassed that it was taking so long. I didn't get my period until I was 14 years old. And when I finally DID get it, I didn't know that it was my period! I imagined that the blood would be bright red as if I had cut my finger. But the blood was much darker, especially at first, and there was not very much of it. I was too embarrassed to talk to my Mum about it (who had never talked to me about periods) and so I called my cousin. She explained to me that what was happening was, in fact, my period. I remember feeling a little excited and proud of it. I had just started wearing my first bra then and with my period, I felt more grown-up. In those early months and first few years, I didn't get my period very regularly. I would skip months and it was tricky to plan. I made sure to keep period supplies in a special zipped pouch in my book-bag so that I was always prepared.

MARYAM MONTAGUE

FOUNDER & EXECUTIVE DIRECTOR, PROJECT SOAR

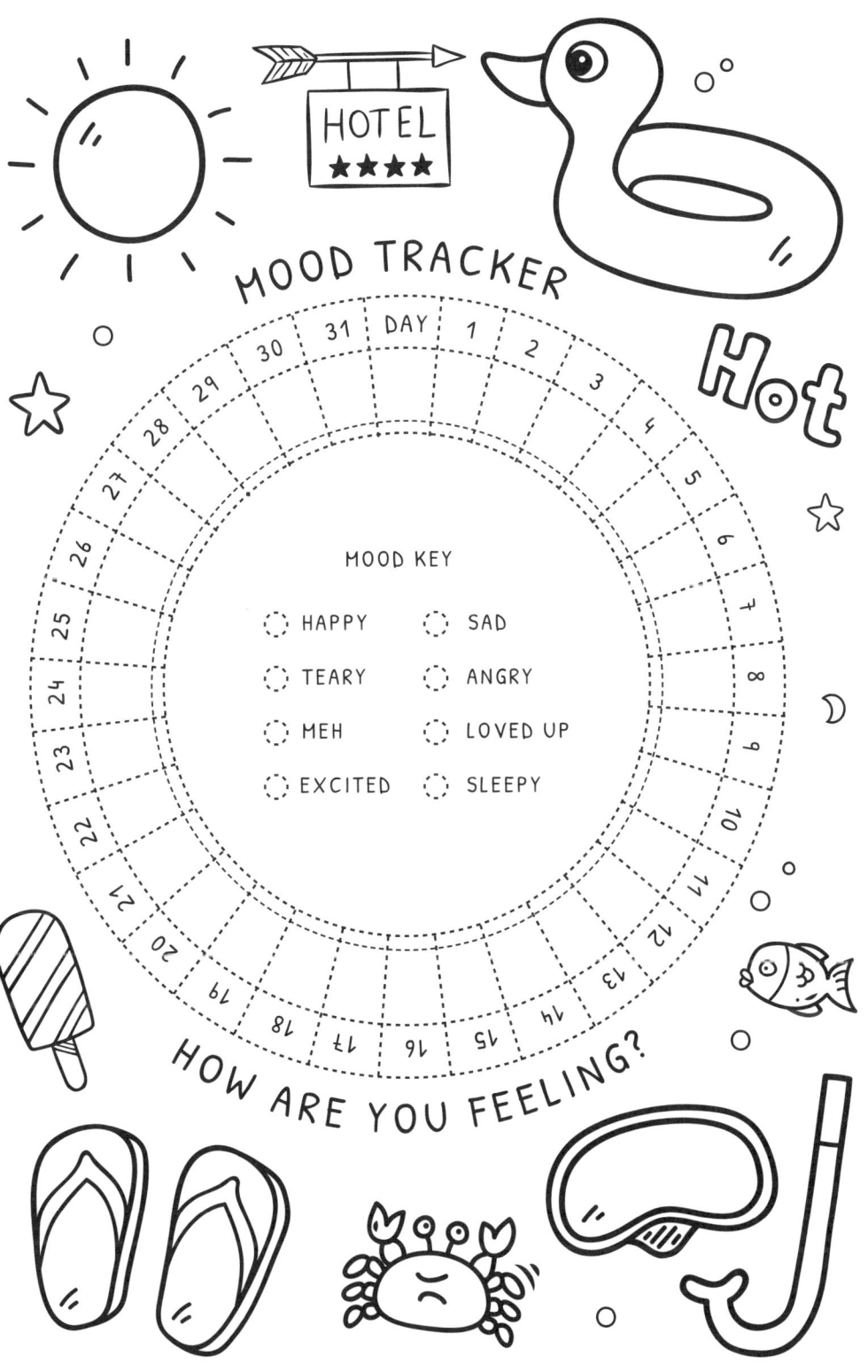

CHAPTER SIX

MONDAY	TUESDAY	WEDNESDAY

THURSDAY	FRIDAY	

MYTH

MENSTRUAL
BLOOD IS
DIFFERENT FROM
NORMAL BLOOD

Menstrual blood is
normal blood. The
same blood that runs
through the rest of
your body.

SATURDAY	SUNDAY

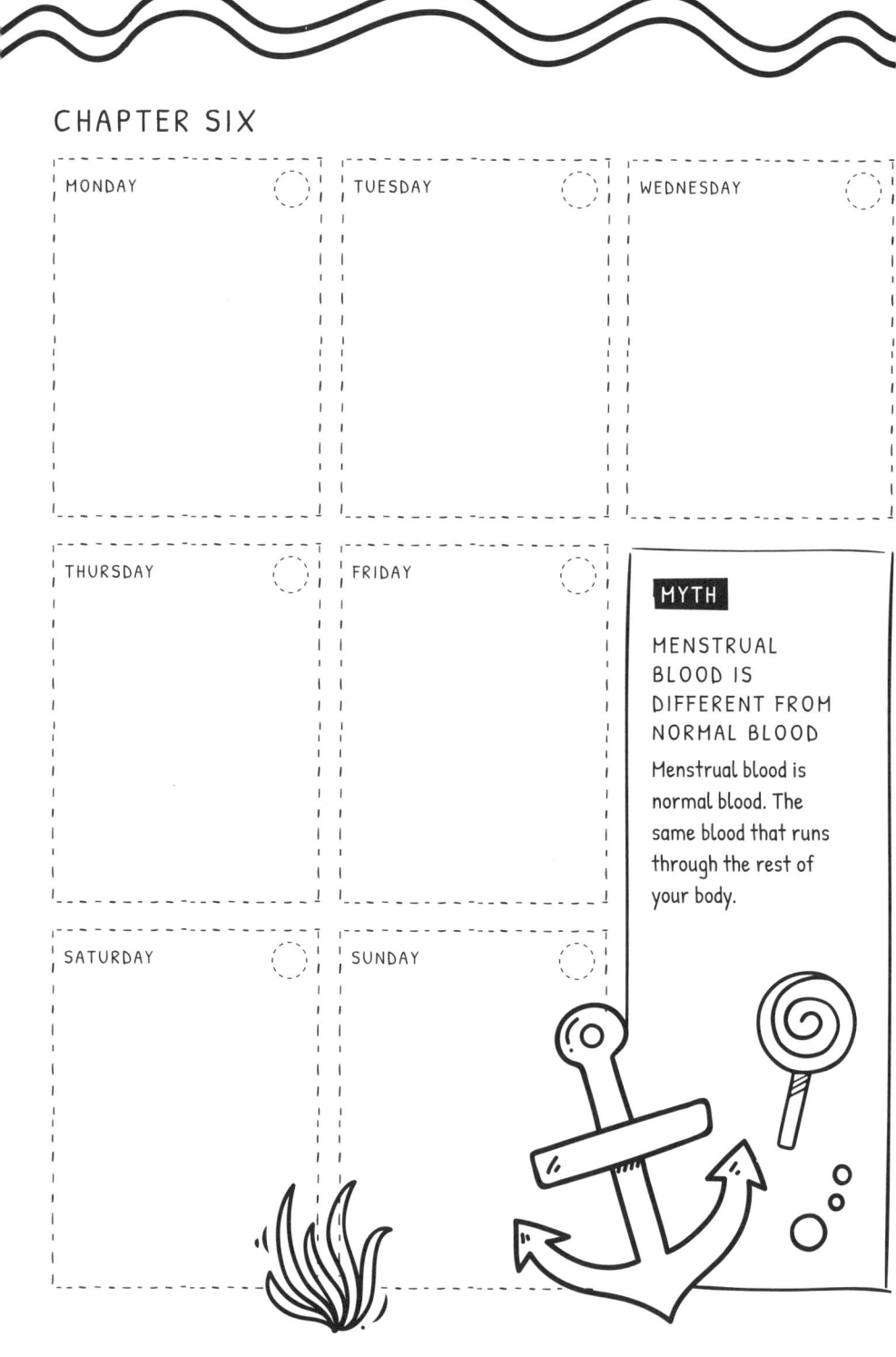

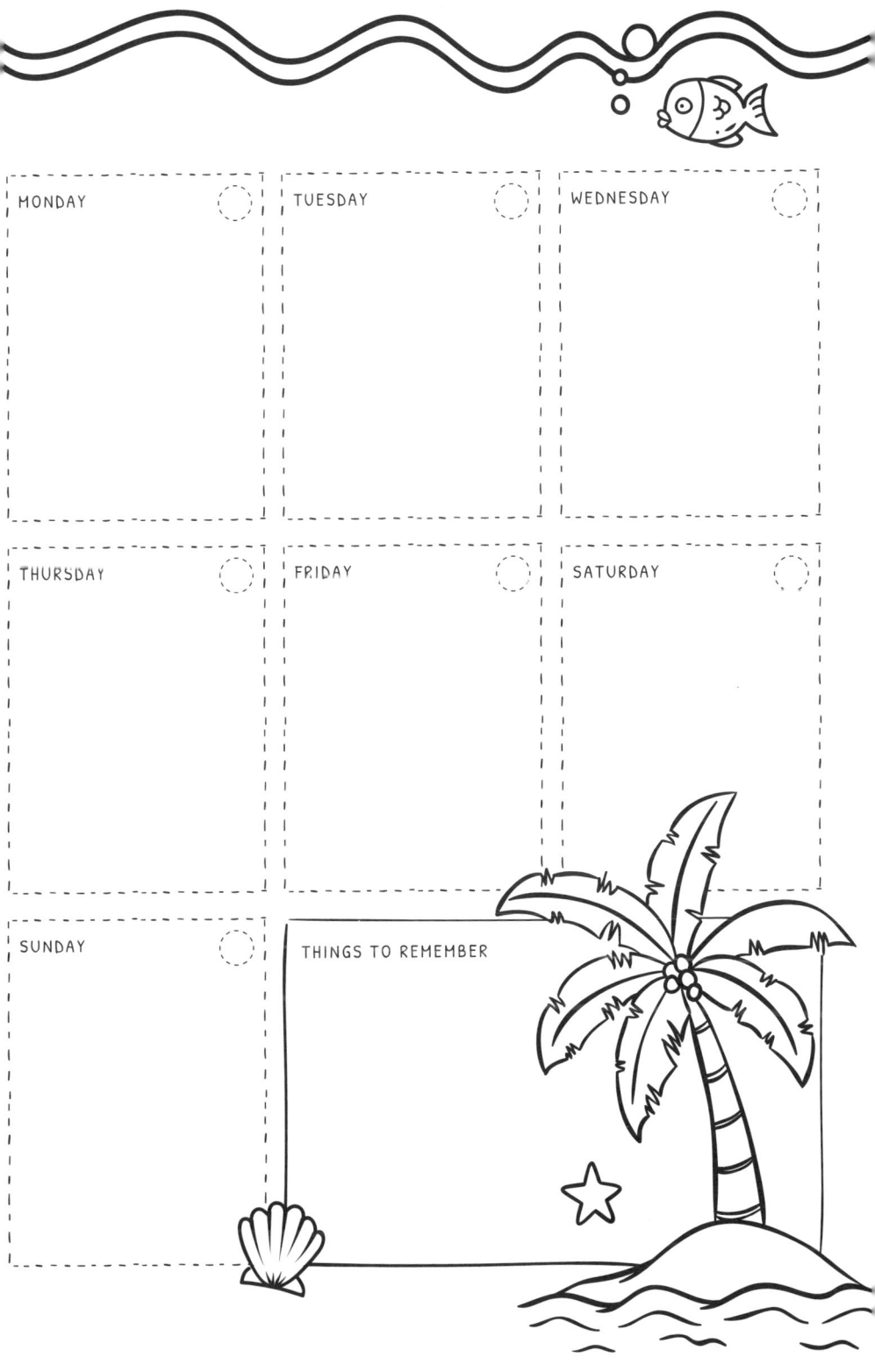

MONDAY

TUESDAY

WEDNESDAY

THURSDAY

FRIDAY

SATURDAY

SUNDAY

THINGS TO REMEMBER

CHAPTER SIX

MONDAY	TUESDAY	WEDNESDAY

THURSDAY	FRIDAY	NOTES

SATURDAY	SUNDAY	

HOW'S YOUR WEEK GOING?

MONDAY ○

TUESDAY ○

WEDNESDAY ○

THURSDAY ○

FRIDAY ○

SATURDAY ○

SUNDAY ○

TIP CUT DOWN ON CAFFEINE

Caffeine is found in most fizzy and hot drinks, and it causes your body to retain water. This will make you feel more bloated and worsen cramps so try your best to avoid caffeine where you can.

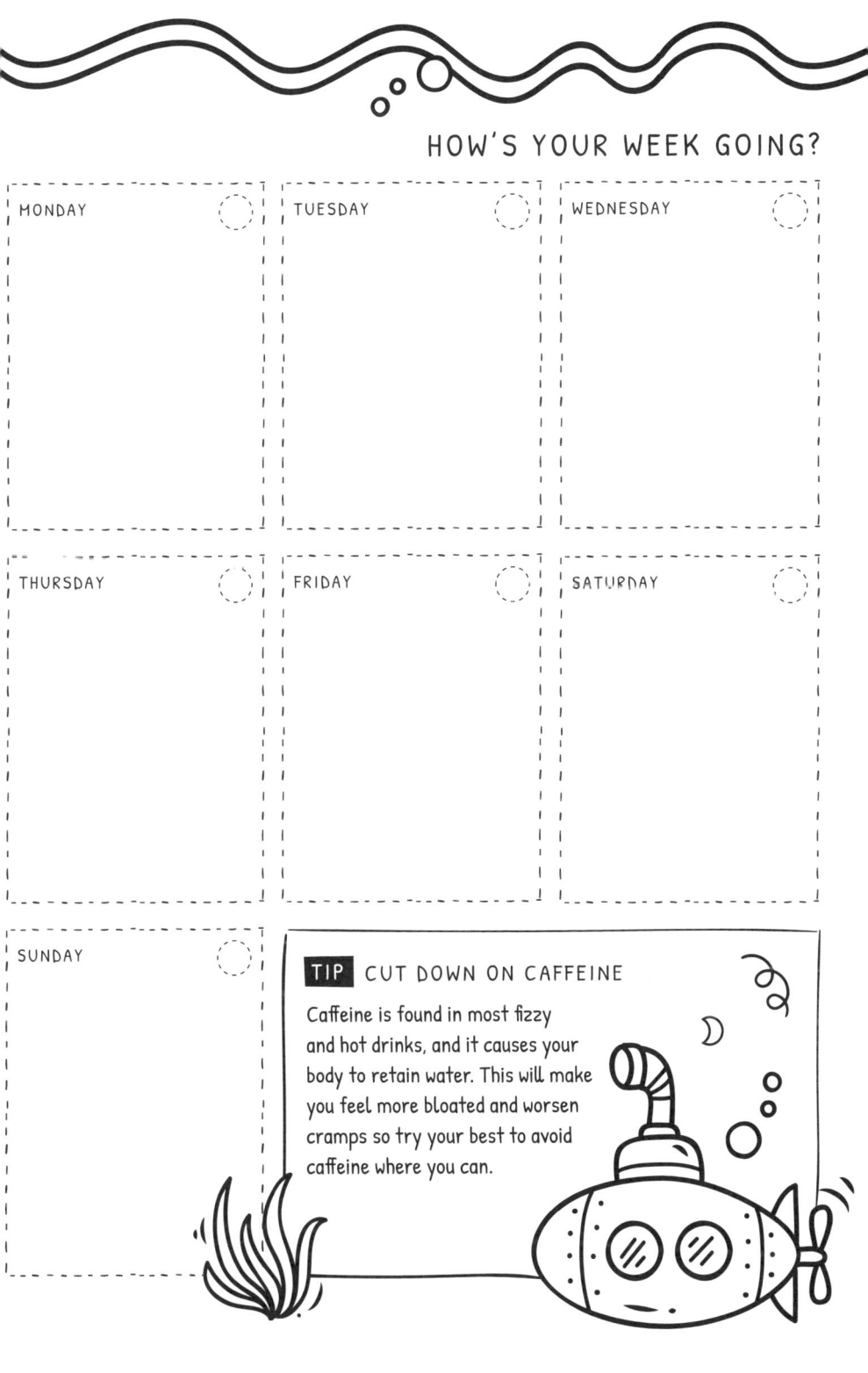

MONDAY

TUESDAY

WEDNESDAY

THURSDAY

FRIDAY

NOTES

SATURDAY

SUNDAY

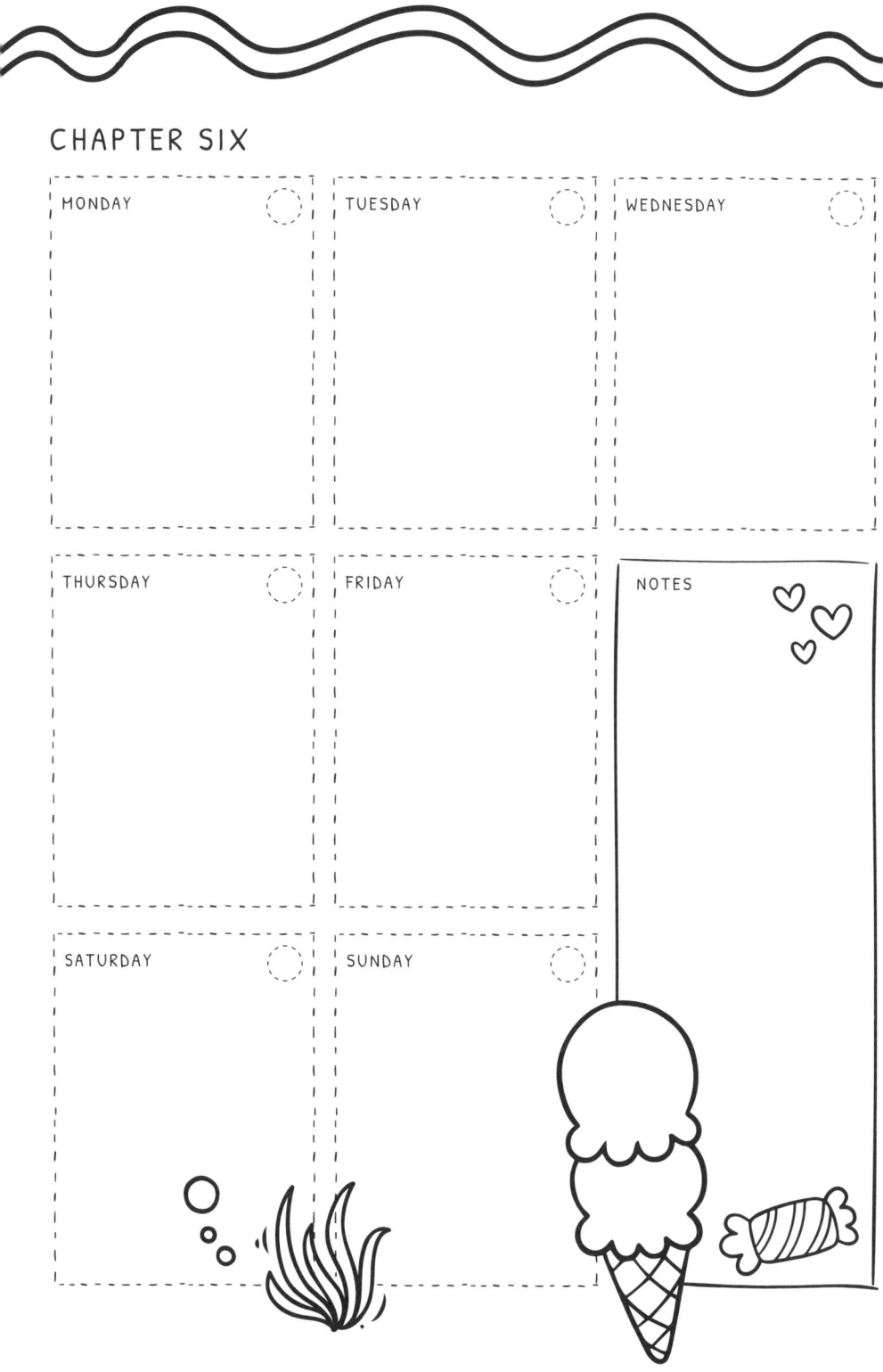

TO DO

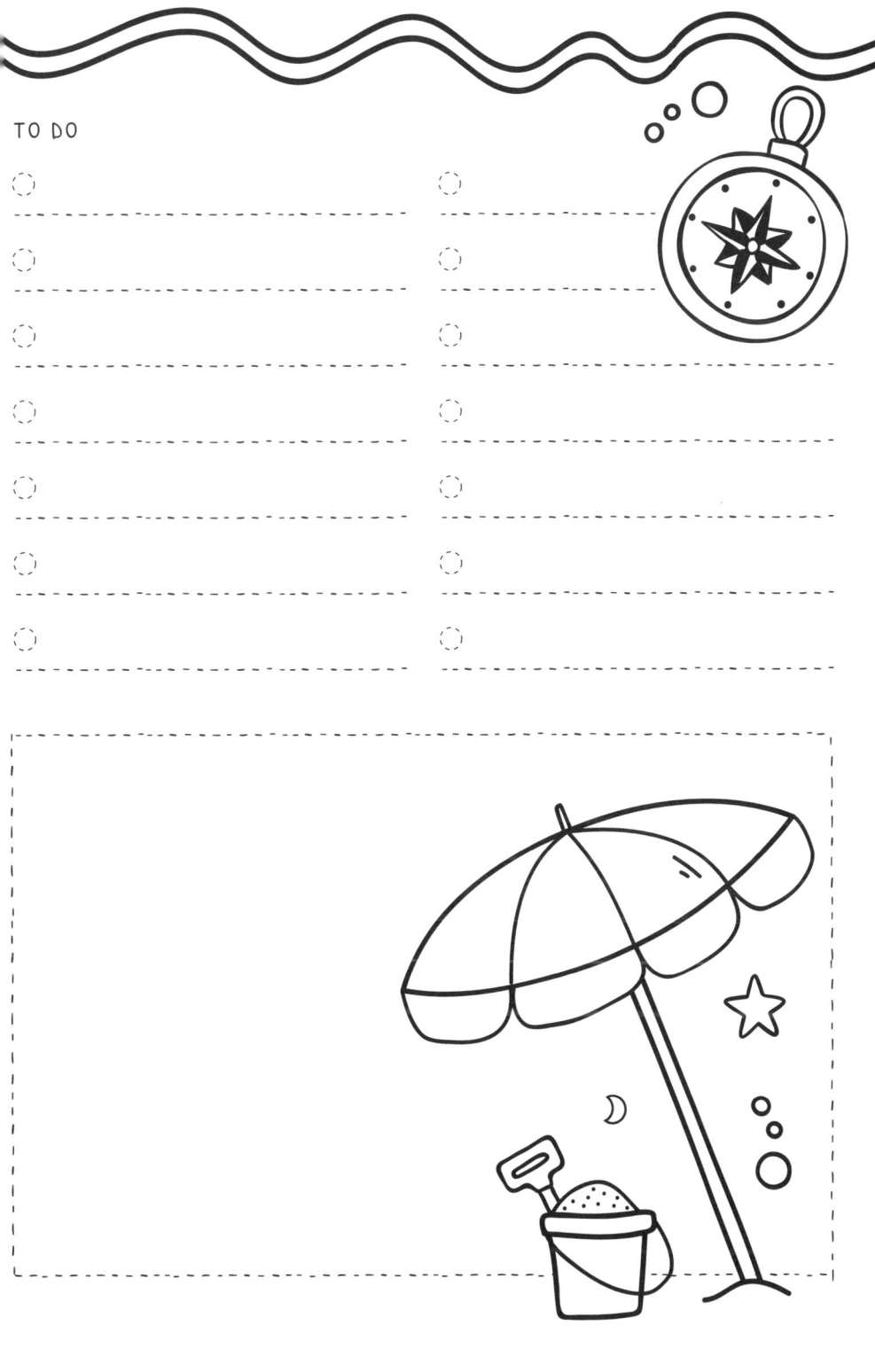

BE KIND TO YOURSELF ALWAYS

You may have days where you feel irritable, stressed, anxious or sad. Remember, it's completely normal to experience these feelings from time to time. When you feel like this, it's important to be kind to yourself and practise self-care. Use the Self-Care Bingo as a reminder of what you can do to look after your wellbeing, and also remember to keep up the basics like eating regular meals, drinking lots of water, looking after your personal hygiene and getting at least 8 hours of sleep a night.

Remember, if you are struggling with stress or anxiety, you should seek help from your parents, guardians or GP.

'If there's anything that particularly strikes me about my period these days, it's that I don't hate having it anymore. I'm 34 and I've been having my period for about 20 years now.

Let's face it, periods aren't that much fun at all. That never changes. But, I think there is something to be said about getting to a place where you can appreciate it. Appreciating all that your body does, including the menstruation cycle, is a form of self-love. In a world that teaches us to mostly be ashamed of, and inconvenienced by, our period, there is no greater rebellion than doing and feeling the opposite. When you bleed, take the time to slow down and get a little self-indulgent while your body does its magic. Drench yourself in love. I can't remember exactly when it changed but I found that when I started thinking of my period in a more appreciative way, it became kinder to me. Try it.'

— DOMINIQUE TIPPER, ACTRESS

SELF-CARE **BINGO**

ADD YOUR OWN

TRIED SOMETHING NEW	GAVE SOMEONE A HUG		MESSAGED A FRIEND	PLAYED A GAME
ATE A YUMMY TREAT	DID SOME YOGA	LISTENED TO MUSIC	WENT TO BED ON TIME	
DID SOME EXERCISE	DID A FUN CRAFT		HAD A SHOWER OR BATH	WATCHED A FILM
LAUGHED A LOT	PAINTED MY NAILS	ATE ALL MY GREENS	READ A NEW BOOK	GAVE MYSELF A COMPLIMENT
WROTE A GRATITUDE LIST	DRANK LOTS OF WATER	WENT FOR A WALK	HAD A FACE MASK	

'Self-care, ultimately, is about taking the time to be comfortable and know yourself. In order for your self-care strategy to be tailor-made for you, work out what brings you peace. What gives you comfort? Start from there. For me, it's a solo trip to an art gallery. Time with my thoughts amongst beautiful art.'

– ANN AKIN, ACTRESS

chapter seven

When I started my period aged 12, it was an uncomfortable conversation for me to have with my mum. I remember her handing me a pad without much explanation other than that she advised me not to use a tampon until I was older. I had terrible periods - long and painful for many years - and believed this was normal and just something I should accept - because no one ever told me otherwise. Now I'm a mother, I've made sure periods are an open and honest conversation in my house for my two young girls - and son - so when the girls start theirs, no topic will be taboo and they will be comfortable talking openly about their experiences.

DEBORAH JOSEPH
EDITOR-IN-CHIEF, GLAMOUR MAGAZINE

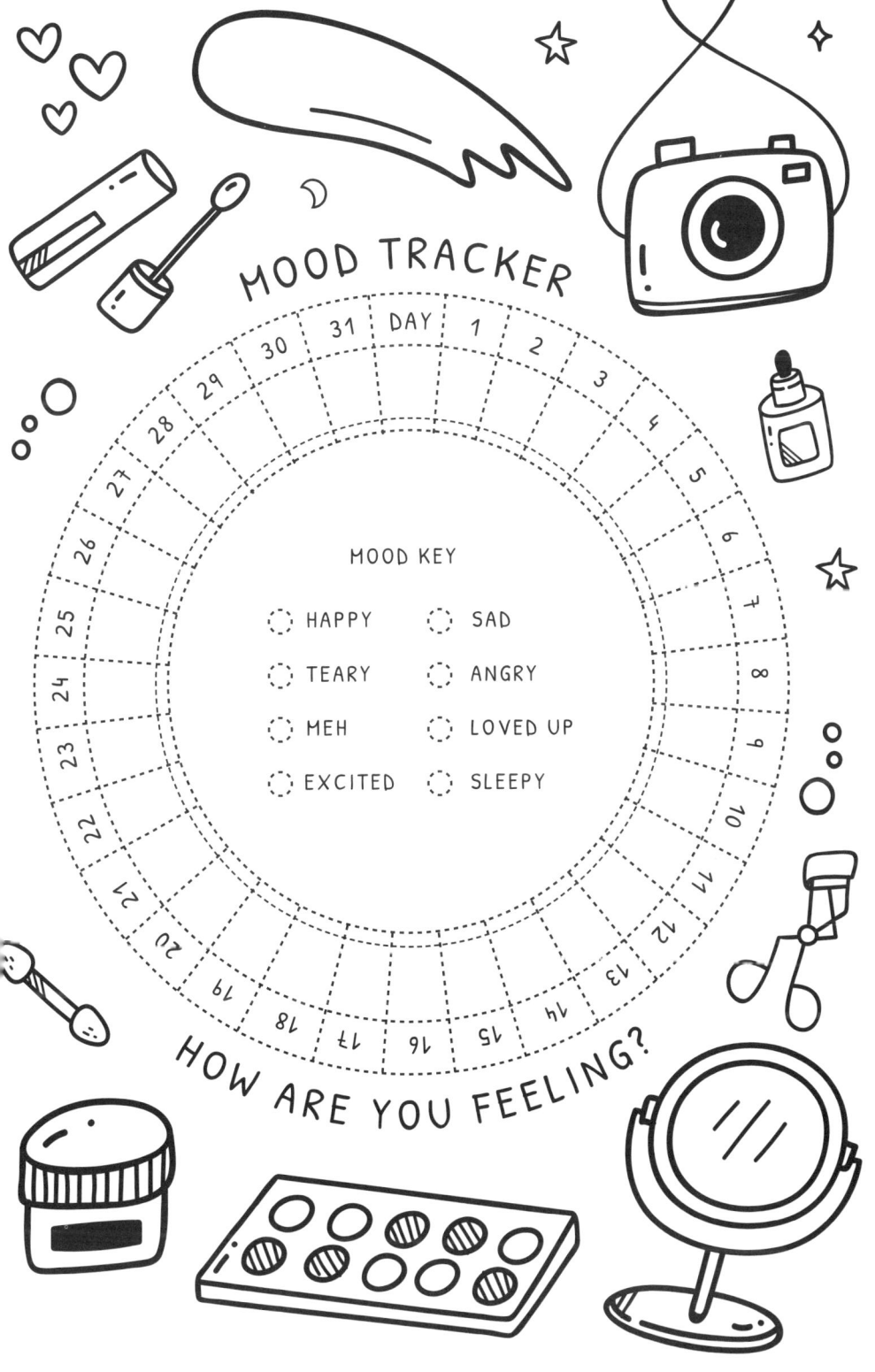

MOOD TRACKER

30 31 DAY 1 2 3 4 5 6 7 8 9 10 11 12 13 14 15 16 17 18 19 20 21 22 23 24 25 26 27 28 29

MOOD KEY

○ HAPPY   ○ SAD

○ TEARY   ○ ANGRY

○ MEH   ○ LOVED UP

○ EXCITED   ○ SLEEPY

HOW ARE YOU FEELING?

CHAPTER SEVEN

MONDAY	TUESDAY	WEDNESDAY

THURSDAY	FRIDAY

MYTH

EVERYONE HAS THE SAME PERIOD FLOW

Not everyone has the same period flow; some can be light and some can be heavier. On average we lose 30-40 ml of blood during our period, which is about 2-3 tablespoons; however, periods can be heavier than this. You'll soon start to understand what a normal flow for your body is. Use the period tracker to see what your cycle is like.

SATURDAY	SUNDAY

MONDAY ○

TUESDAY ○

WEDNESDAY ○

THURSDAY ○

FRIDAY ○

SATURDAY ○

SUNDAY ○

THINGS TO REMEMBER

MONDAY	TUESDAY	WEDNESDAY

THURSDAY	FRIDAY	NOTES

SATURDAY	SUNDAY	

HOW'S YOUR WEEK GOING?

MONDAY

TUESDAY

WEDNESDAY

THURSDAY

FRIDAY

SATURDAY

SUNDAY

TIP KEEP HYDRATED

When you feel bloated the last thing you'll feel like will be to drink plenty of water. Remember, being dehydrated can make you feel worse and can make your cramps more painful, so try and drink 2 litres of water a day to keep hydrated.

CHAPTER SEVEN

MONDAY

TUESDAY

WEDNESDAY

THURSDAY

FRIDAY

NOTES

SATURDAY

SUNDAY

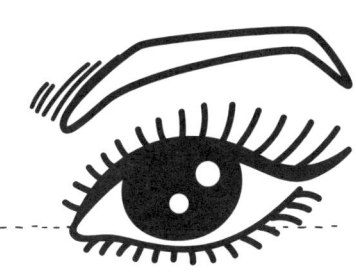

TO DO

◌
- -

◌
- -

◌
- -

◌
- -

◌
- -

◌
- -

◌
- -

◌
- -

◌
- -

◌
- -

◌
- -

◌
- -

◌
- -

◌
- -

MAKE UP

CHAPTER eight

I got my period at thirteen years old. Prior to this moment, I knew just two facts about periods; they involve blood and they mark a girl's entry into womanhood. I was fine with the blood; as the oldest sister of three boys I had been scratched, wrestled and tripped over more than most girls my age and if anything it seemed rather exciting. I wasn't fine with the 'being a woman' part. Womanhood was a foreign country, one I was highly uninterested in visiting. Did this blood between my legs mean I had to learn what taxes were? Did a tampon come with a mortgage? As my monthly bleed came around would I be made to start sipping wine and doing Pilates? I decided that if no one knew about my period, then no one would make me grow up faster than I was ready to. I shoved a pad into my pants, swallowed my secret, and left my kind, worried mother completely in the dark. Looking back I want to scoop up this spotty pre-teen and tell her it's ok. I want to tell her that blood is just blood. I want to tell her that it's a bodily function, not a dark omen of adulthood. I want to tell her that in a decade's time she still won't know what it means to be a woman and that's OK. I want to tell her about period pain, paracetamol and hot water bottles. I want to tell her that boys bleed too sometimes. I want to tell her nothing's changed. Maybe I can tell you that instead.

SCARLETT CURTIS
DIRECTOR, SCARLETTCURTIS.COM

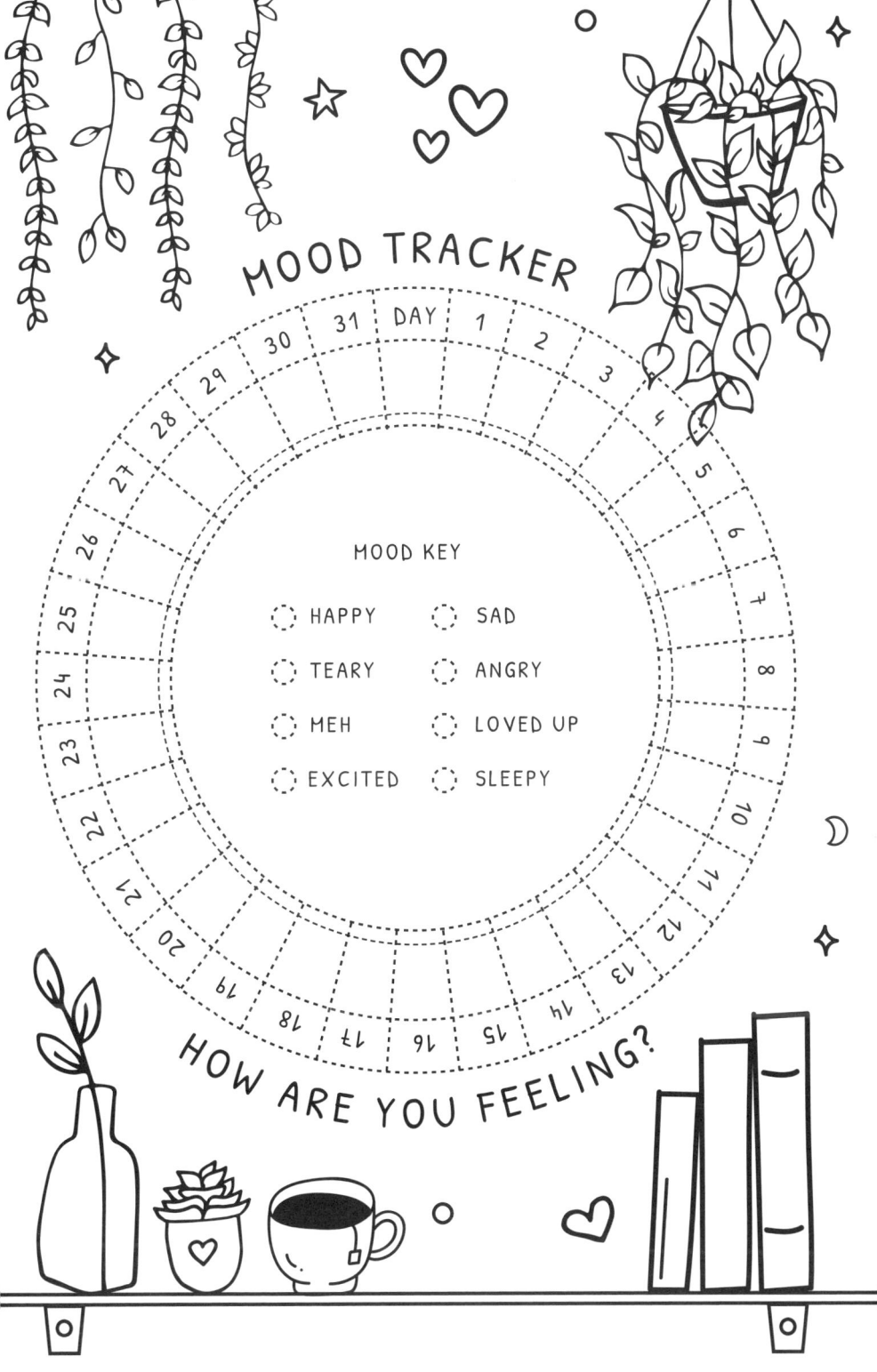

MONDAY

TUESDAY

WEDNESDAY

THURSDAY

FRIDAY

MYTH

EXERCISING DURING YOUR PERIOD IS BAD FOR YOU

Exercise can actually help ease cramps and menstrual symptoms, so feel free to get moving – do some gentle exercise like yoga or go and play your normal sport.

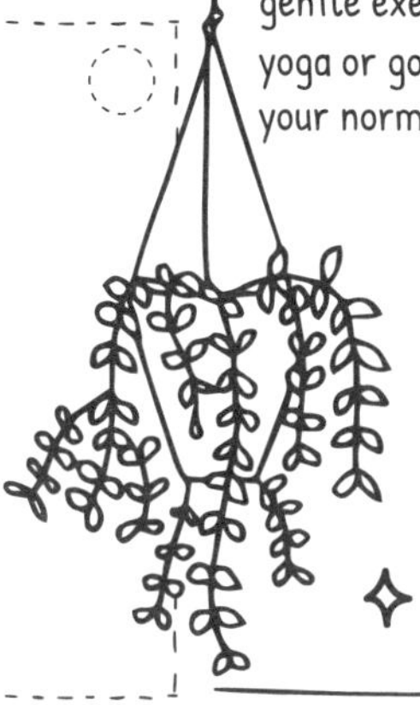

SATURDAY

SUNDAY

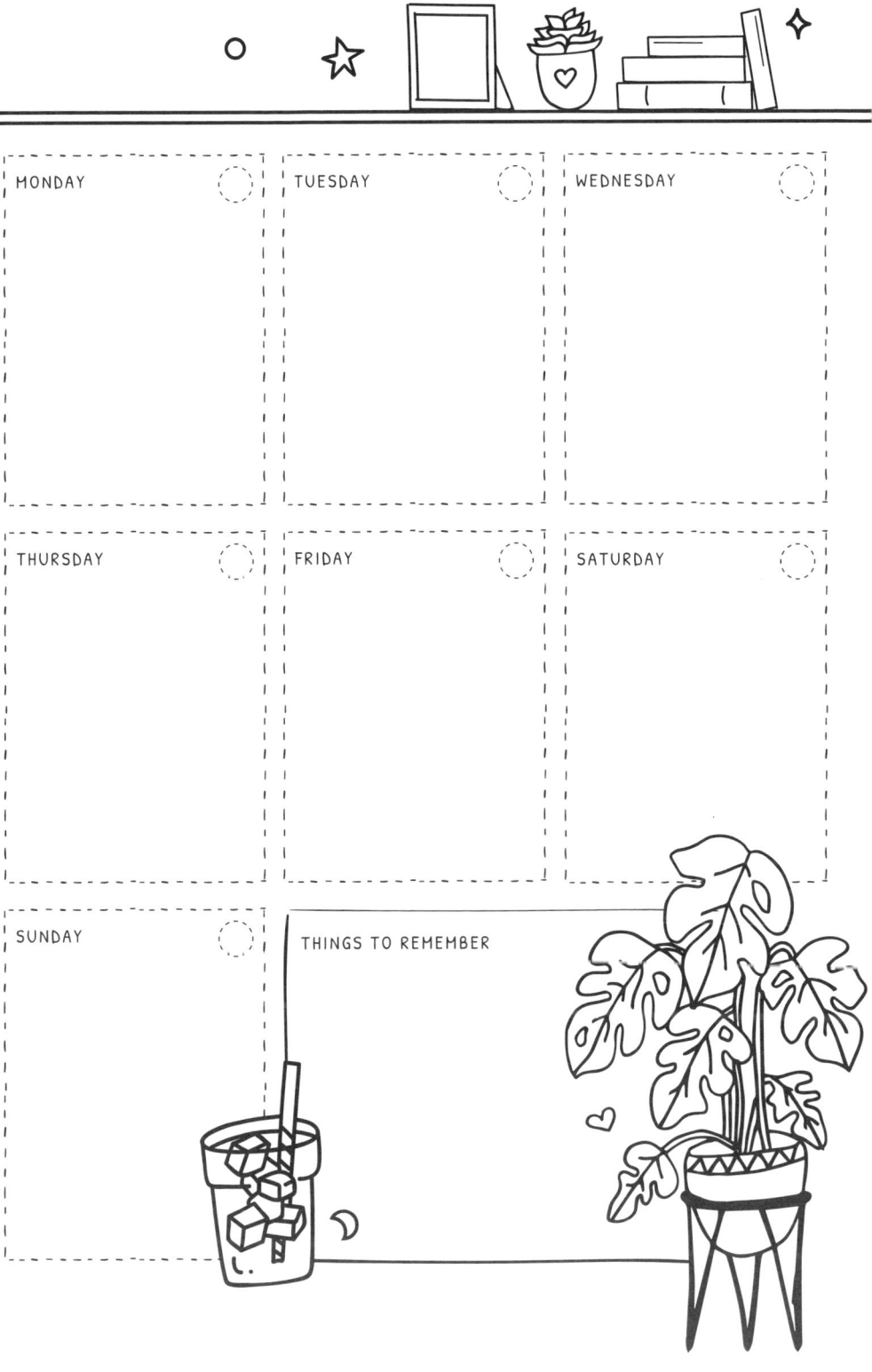

MONDAY

TUESDAY

WEDNESDAY

THURSDAY

FRIDAY

SATURDAY

SUNDAY

THINGS TO REMEMBER

CHAPTER EIGHT

MONDAY	TUESDAY	WEDNESDAY

THURSDAY	FRIDAY	NOTES

SATURDAY	SUNDAY	

HOW'S YOUR WEEK GOING?

MONDAY

TUESDAY

WEDNESDAY

THURSDAY

FRIDAY

SATURDAY

SUNDAY

TIP REACH FOR THE FRUIT

Salt is another thing that makes your body retain water so resist the urge to snack on that packet of crisps and pick something like a banana or nuts instead (provided you are not allergic to them).

MONDAY

TUESDAY

WEDNESDAY

THURSDAY

FRIDAY

NOTES

SATURDAY

SUNDAY

TO DO

○

○

○

○

○

○

○

○

○

○

○

○

○

○

'What makes you different or weird, that's your strength.'

— MERYL STREEP

'Try doing a period meditation. Close your eyes and imagine a warm, healing light bathing your pelvic area. Keep your attention on your breath and imagine this warm light expanding and contracting with your breath. Imagine the light soothing all of your internal organs and belly with each and every breath.'

— MARYAM MONTAGUE

GIRLHOOD
THE STORY

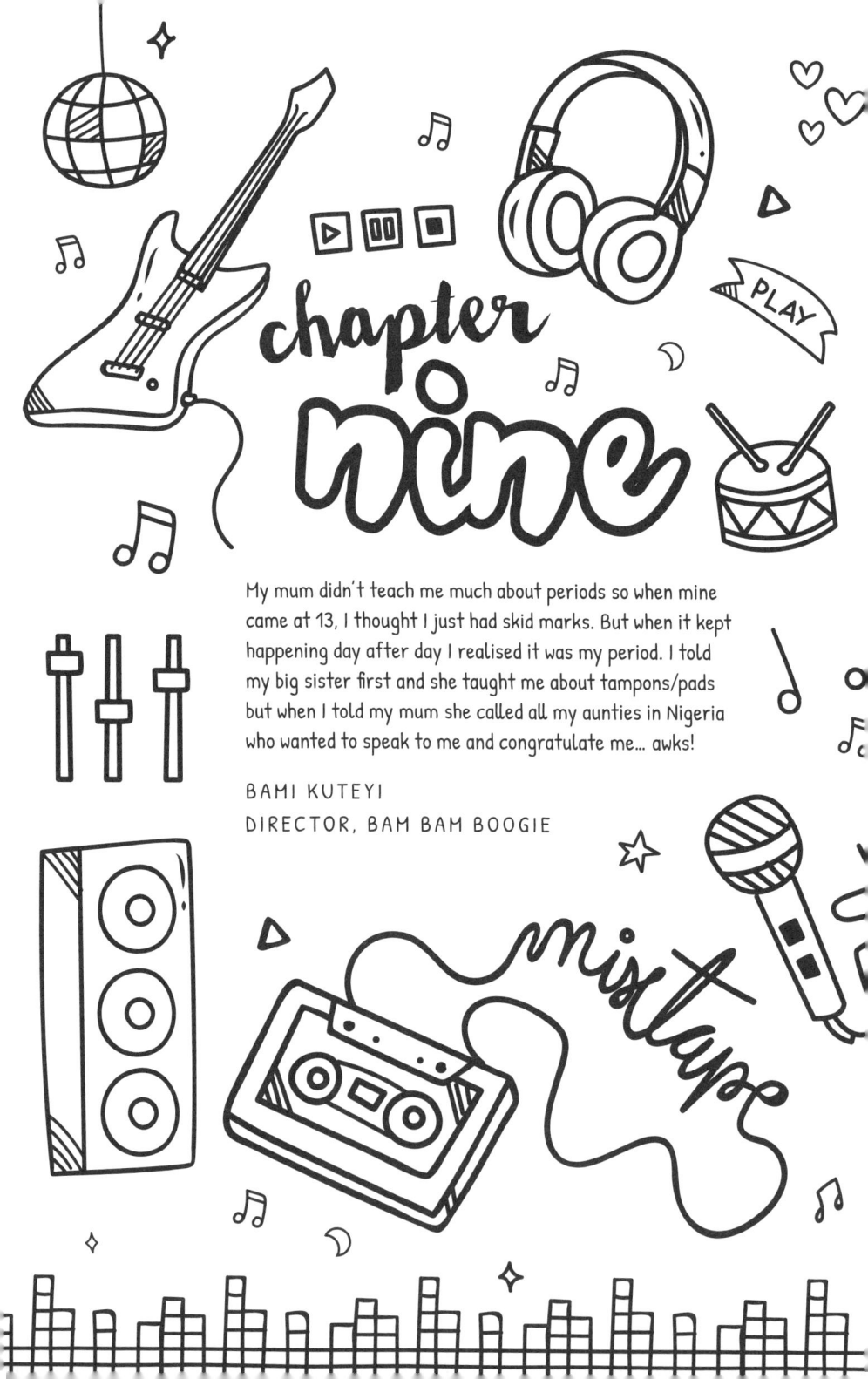

chapter nine

My mum didn't teach me much about periods so when mine came at 13, I thought I just had skid marks. But when it kept happening day after day I realised it was my period. I told my big sister first and she taught me about tampons/pads but when I told my mum she called all my aunties in Nigeria who wanted to speak to me and congratulate me... awks!

BAMI KUTEYI
DIRECTOR, BAM BAM BOOGIE

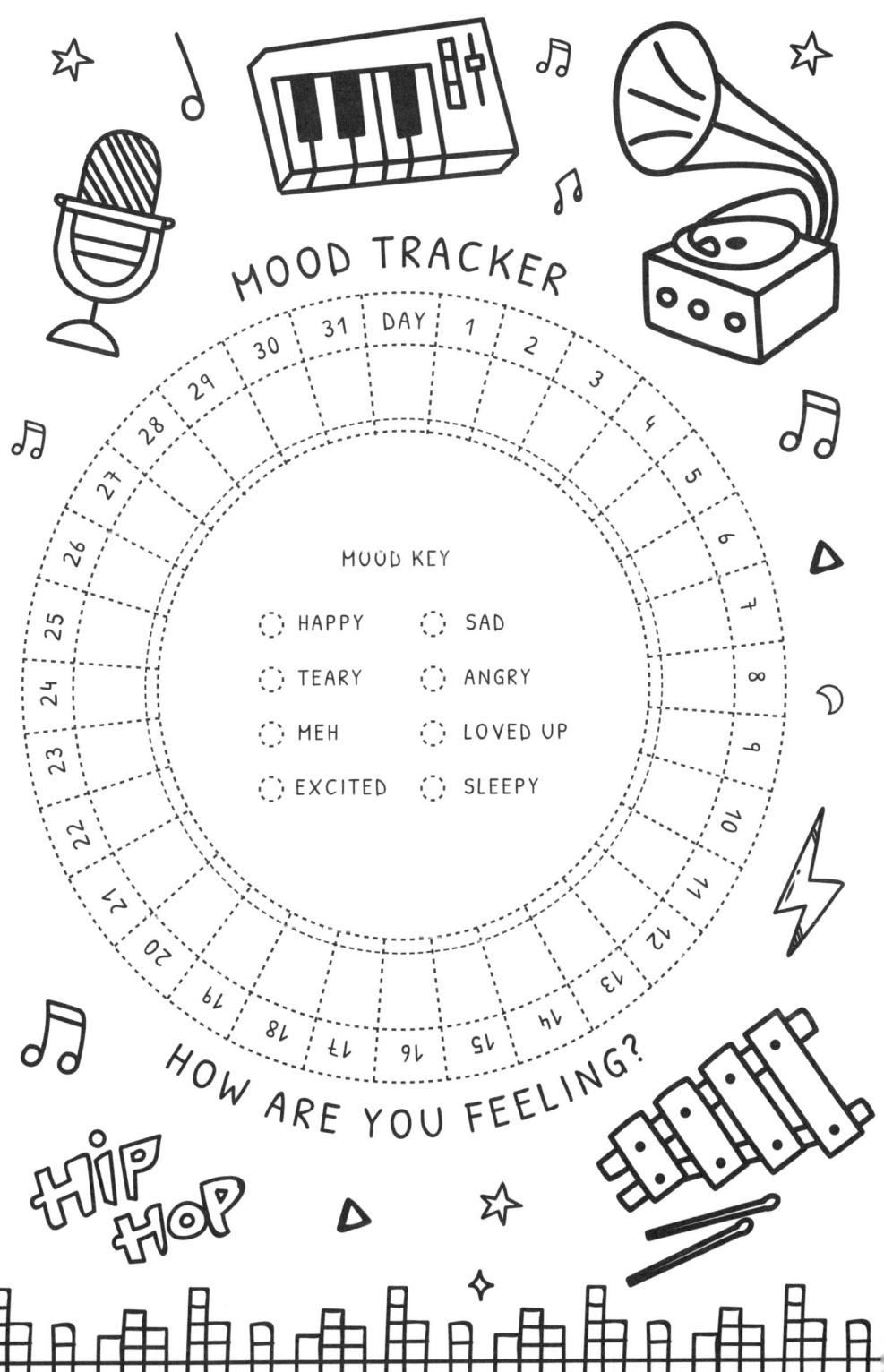

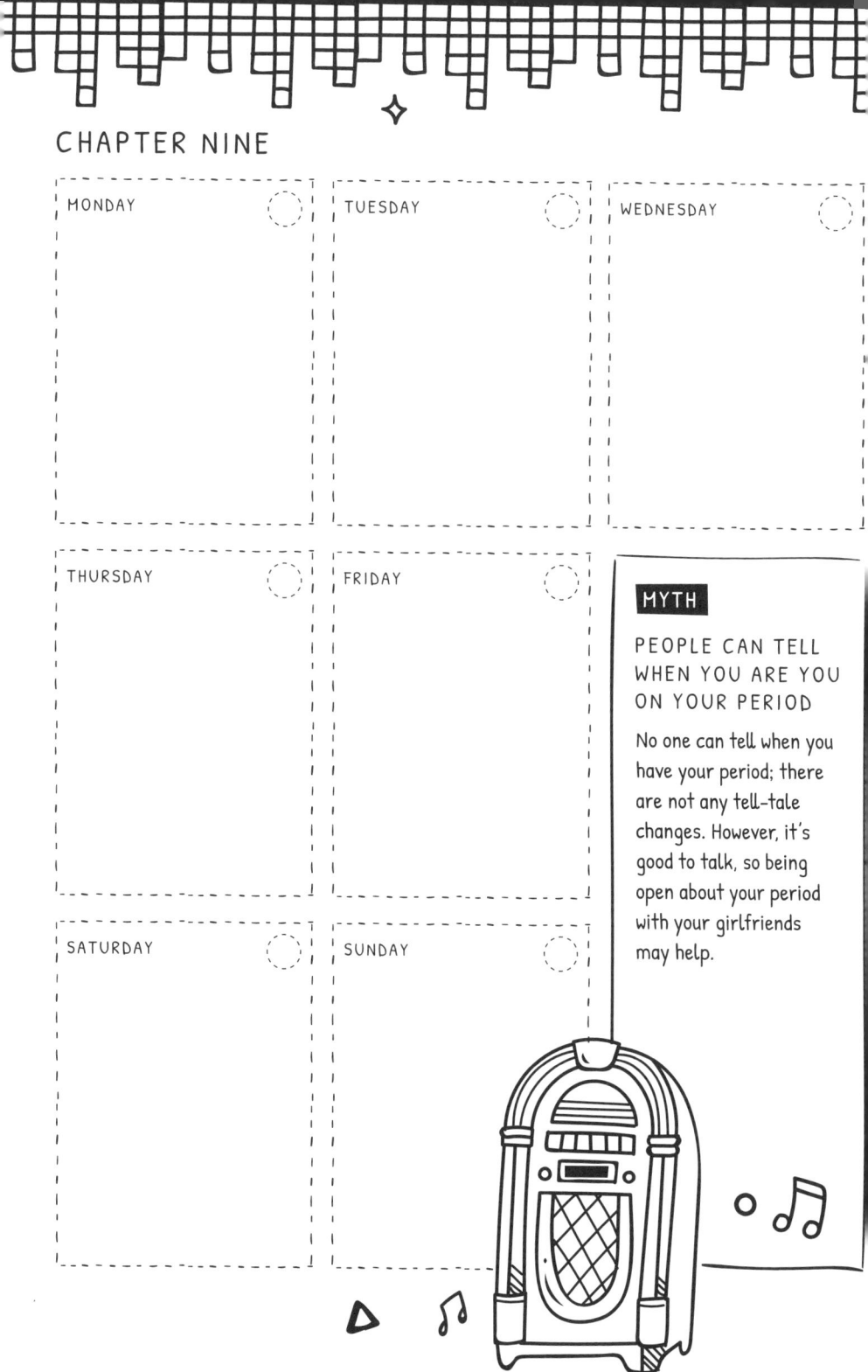

CHAPTER NINE

MONDAY	TUESDAY	WEDNESDAY

THURSDAY	FRIDAY

MYTH

PEOPLE CAN TELL WHEN YOU ARE YOU ON YOUR PERIOD

No one can tell when you have your period; there are not any tell-tale changes. However, it's good to talk, so being open about your period with your girlfriends may help.

SATURDAY	SUNDAY

HOW'S YOUR WEEK GOING?

MONDAY

TUESDAY

WEDNESDAY

THURSDAY

FRIDAY

SATURDAY

SUNDAY

THINGS TO REMEMBER

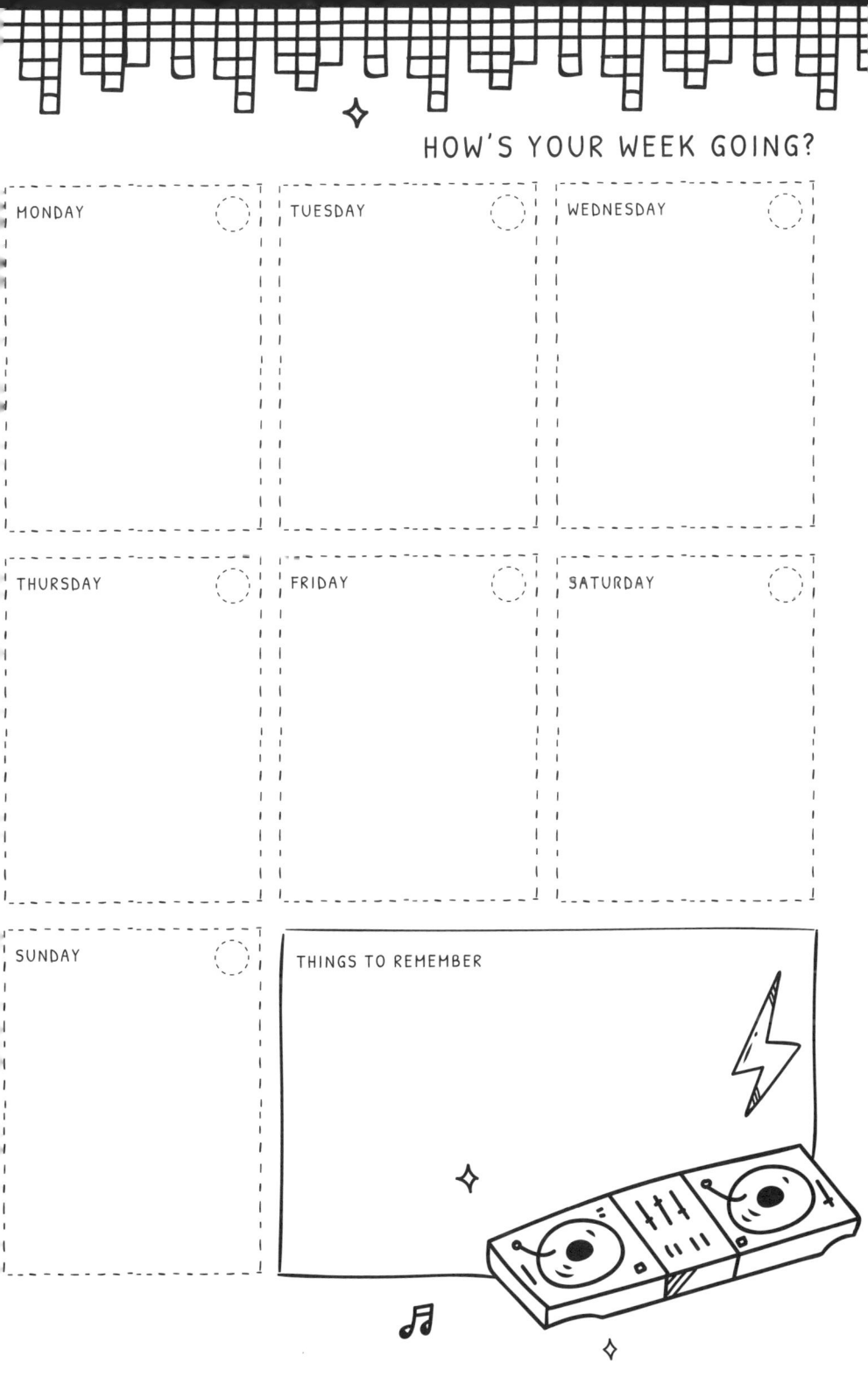

CHAPTER NINE

MONDAY	TUESDAY	WEDNESDAY

THURSDAY	FRIDAY	NOTES

SATURDAY	SUNDAY

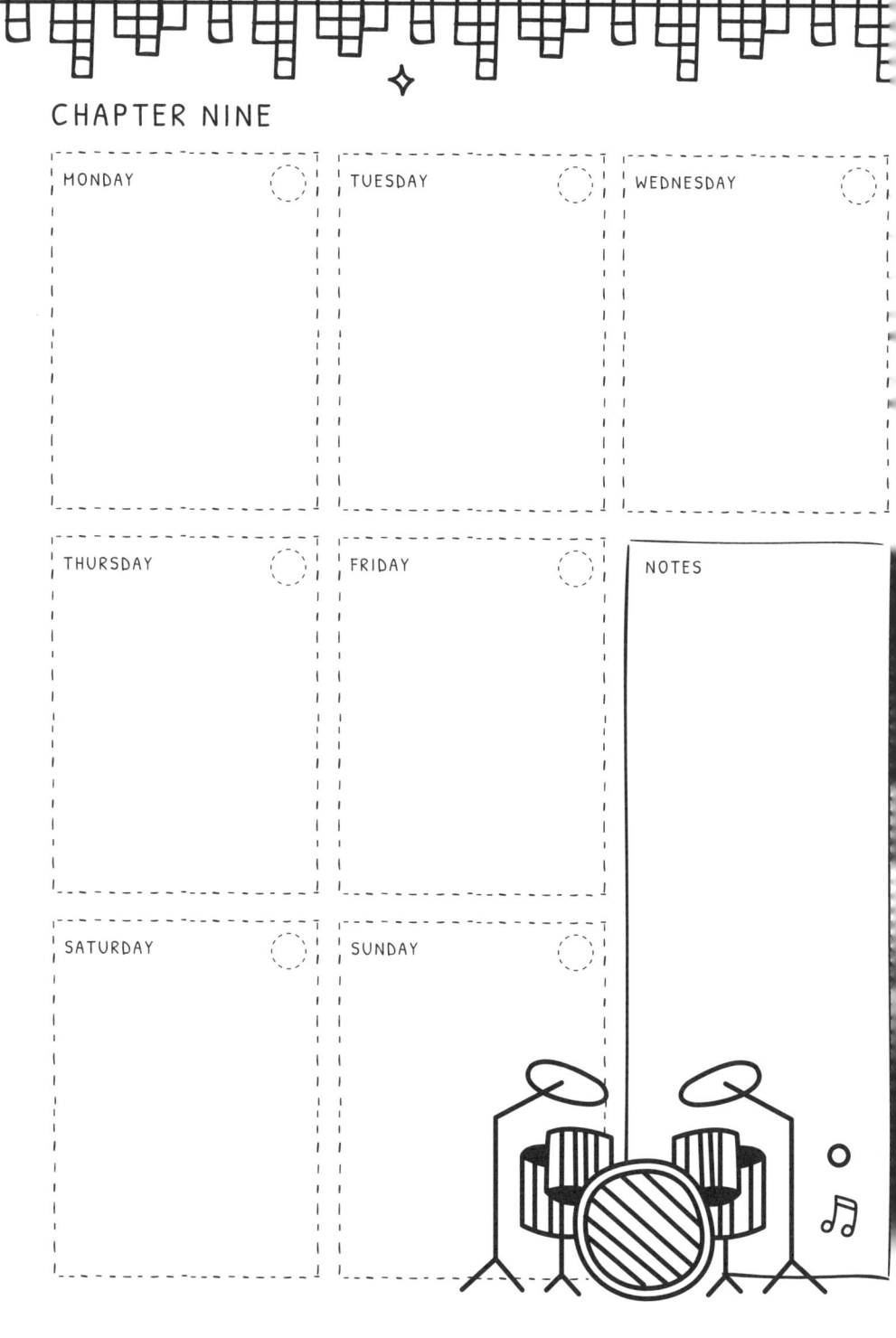

MONDAY

TUESDAY

WEDNESDAY

THURSDAY

FRIDAY

SATURDAY

SUNDAY

TIP EAT MORE GREENS

You'll feel quite tired when on your period as your iron levels will be lower, so try eating more iron-rich foods like dark green vegetables, beans, eggs and dried fruit. Ask your parents to help include more of these in your meals.

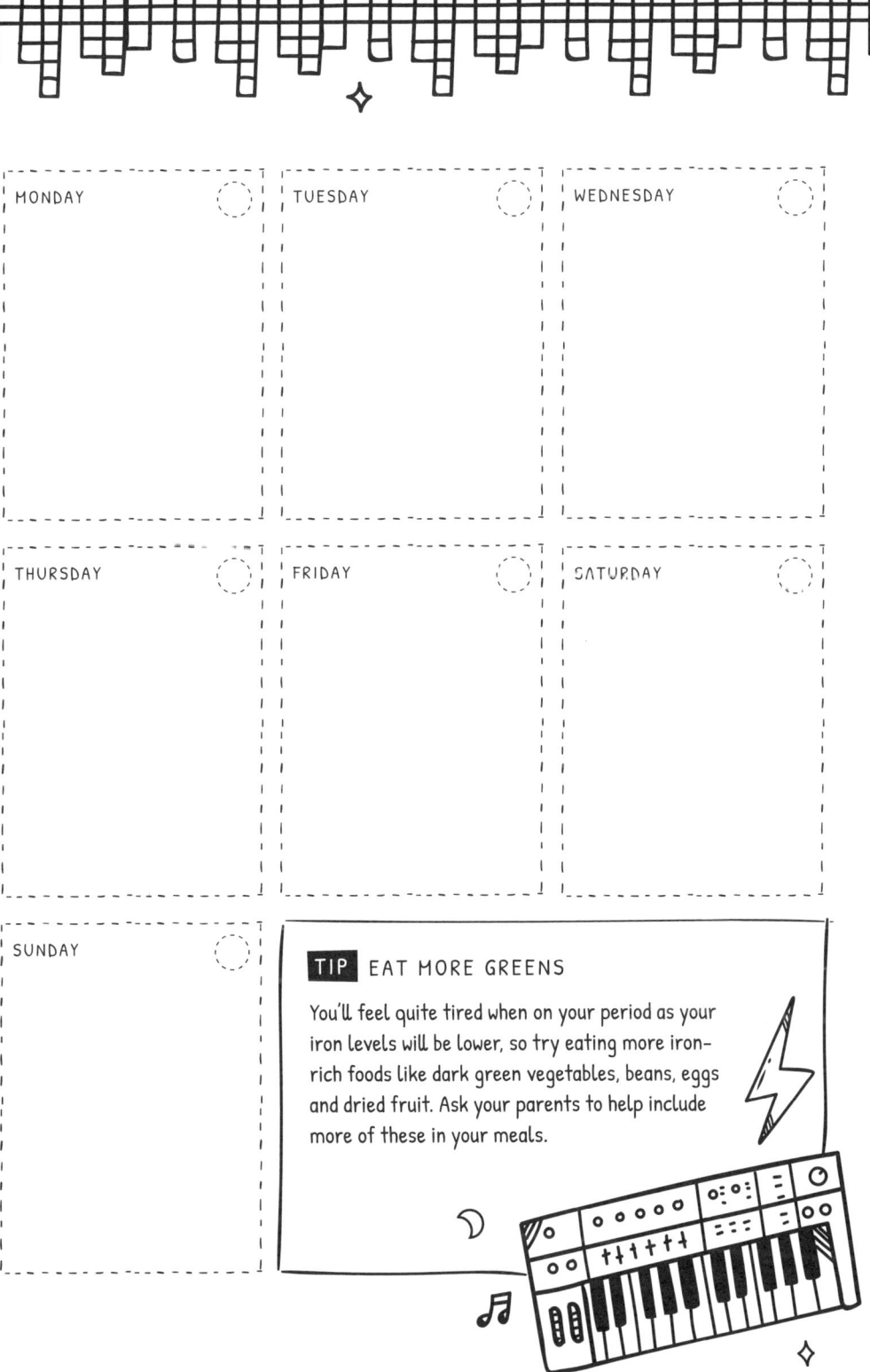

CHAPTER NINE

MONDAY

TUESDAY

WEDNESDAY

THURSDAY

FRIDAY

NOTES

SATURDAY

SUNDAY

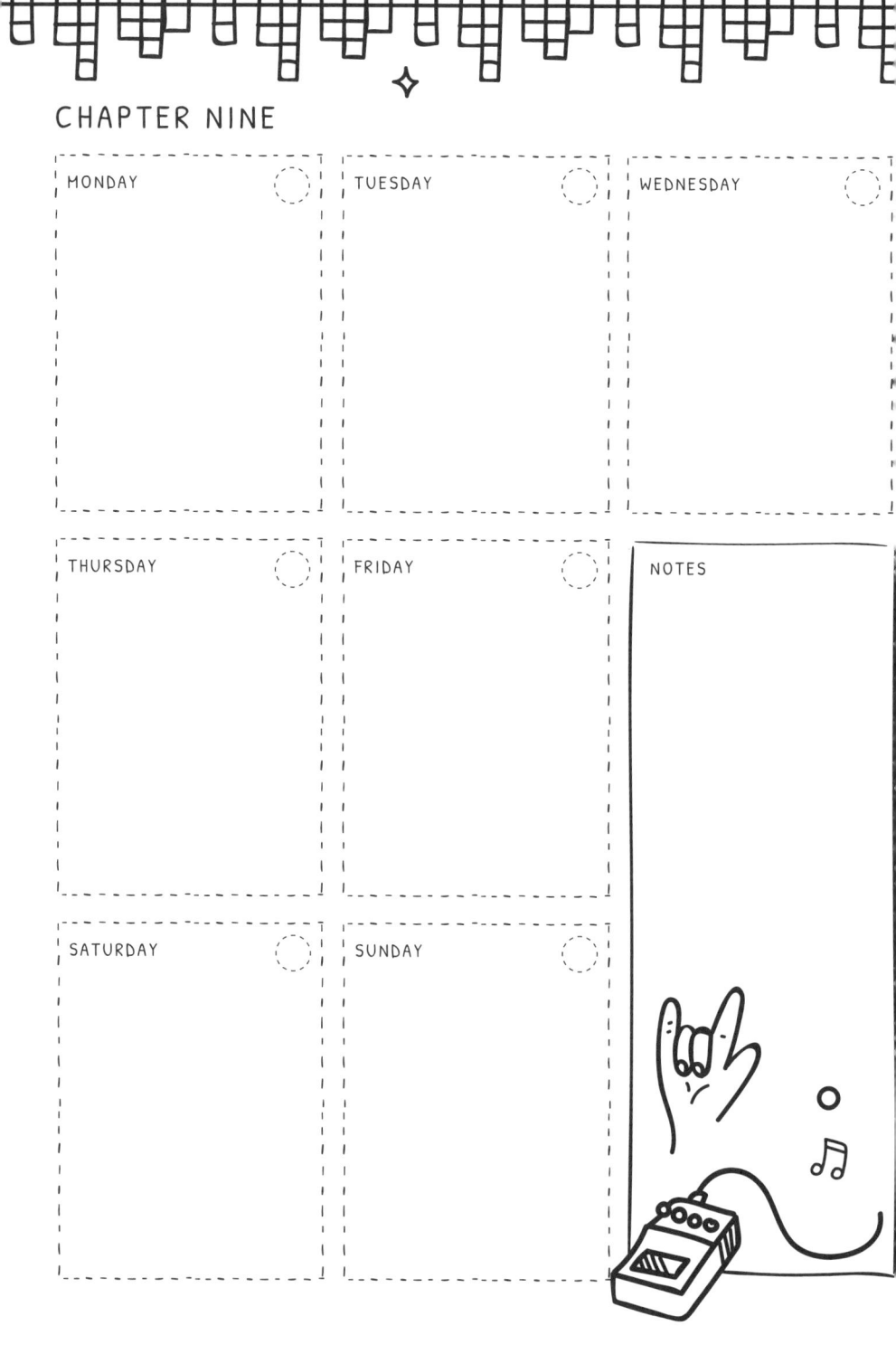

TO DO

'A girl should be two things: who and what she wants.'

— COCO CHANEL

CHAPTER 10

I was 9 when my mum, Rosemary Brennan, tied me to the fence at Greenham Common to campaign for World peace. I don't remember being frightened. Being surrounded by women who were trying to save the world was all I knew as a young girl and there was always so much laughter. I felt safe and free amongst these women. But when I got my period aged 10, we were at a mixed, naturist camping site in the South of France. Mum, overwhelmed with pride and excited by this statement of my womanhood, organised a surprise party fully stocked with Viennetta ice cream, champagne and the entire campsite. She packed me off to the communal showers with a heavy-duty pad. I don't know about now, but back then in the early '80s, camping sites did not have mirrors. They barely had hot water. So I was beyond self-conscious that the sanitary towel would show under my bikini bottoms. Why was I so ashamed? I was 10. I can only imagine it was because it was new and I was very frightened. I wish they taught women about periods at a younger age. And I wish the boys were taught about them too. They are not something to be ashamed of. They should be celebrated! After all, all life - ALL LIFE - comes from the menstrual cycle.

MIKA SIMMONS

ACTRESS, FILMMAKER, HOST OF THE HAPPY VAGINA & FOUNDER LADY GARDEN FOUNDATION

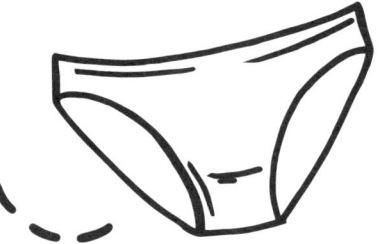

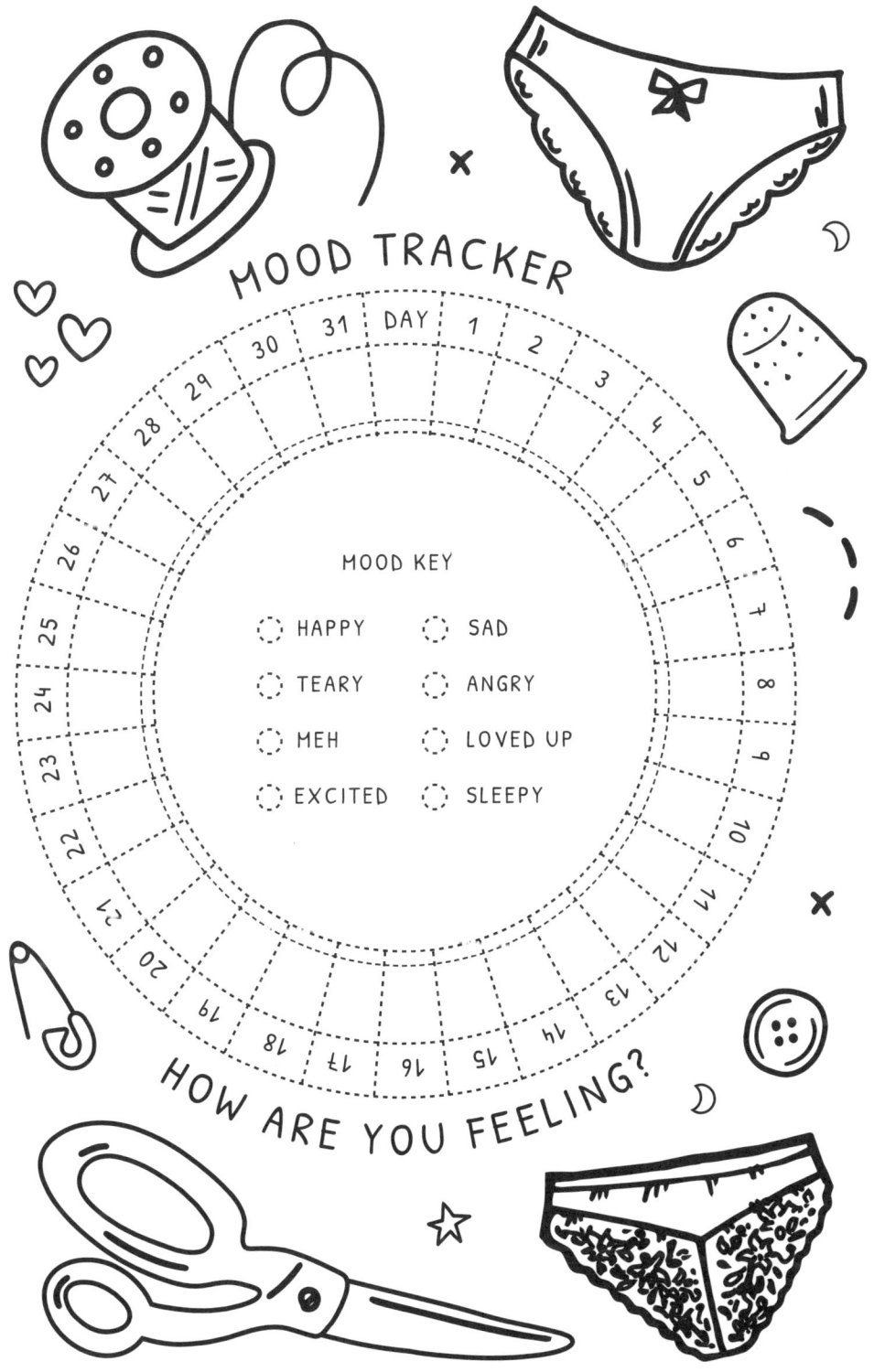

MOOD TRACKER

DAY 1 2 3 4 5 6 7 8 9 10 11 12 13 14 15 16 17 18 19 20 21 22 23 24 25 26 27 28 29 30 31

MOOD KEY

◌ HAPPY   ◌ SAD

◌ TEARY   ◌ ANGRY

◌ MEH   ◌ LOVED UP

◌ EXCITED   ◌ SLEEPY

HOW ARE YOU FEELING?

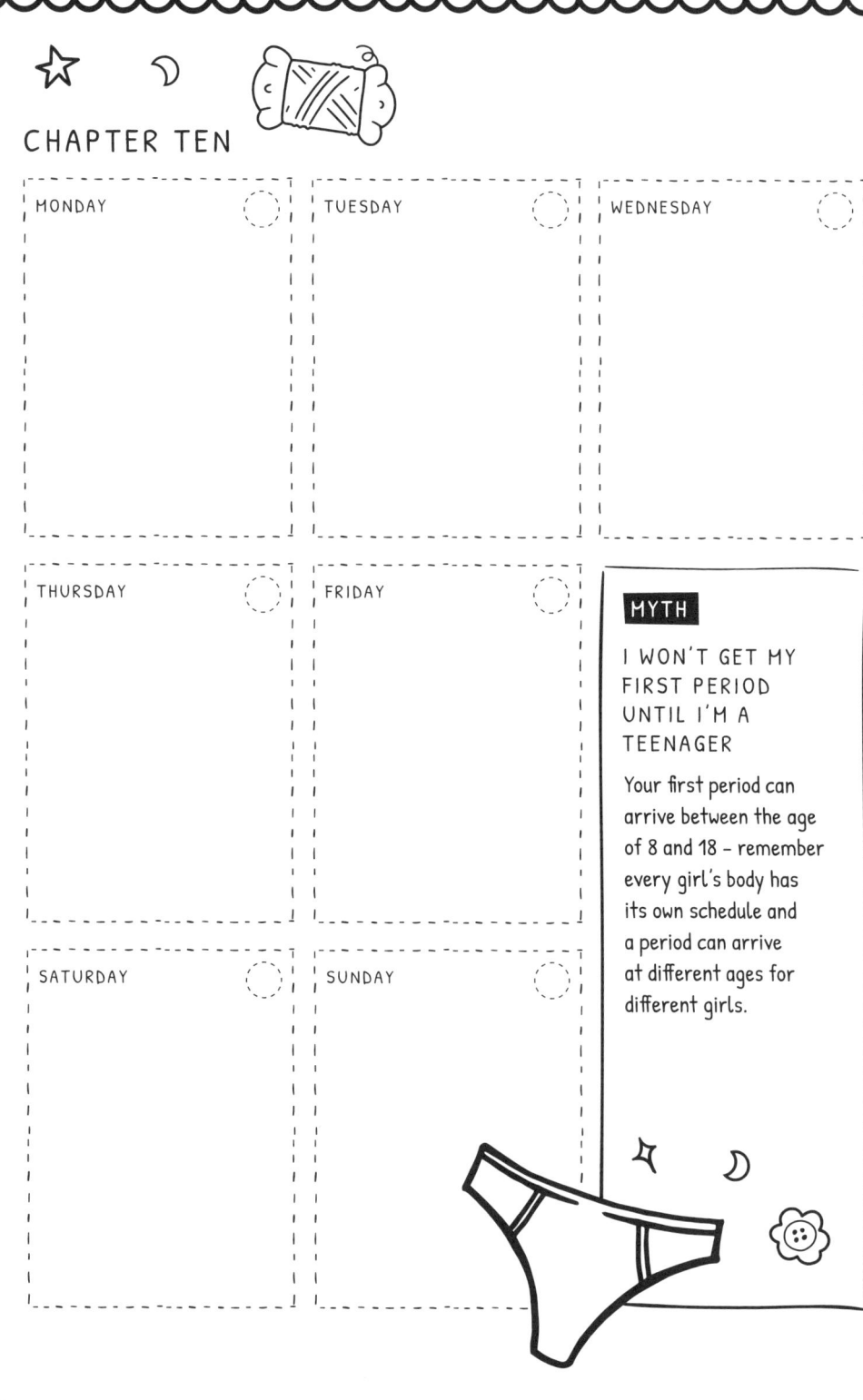

CHAPTER TEN

MONDAY	TUESDAY	WEDNESDAY

THURSDAY	FRIDAY

SATURDAY	SUNDAY

HOW'S YOUR WEEK GOING?

MONDAY

TUESDAY

WEDNESDAY

THURSDAY

FRIDAY

SATURDAY

SUNDAY

THINGS TO REMEMBER

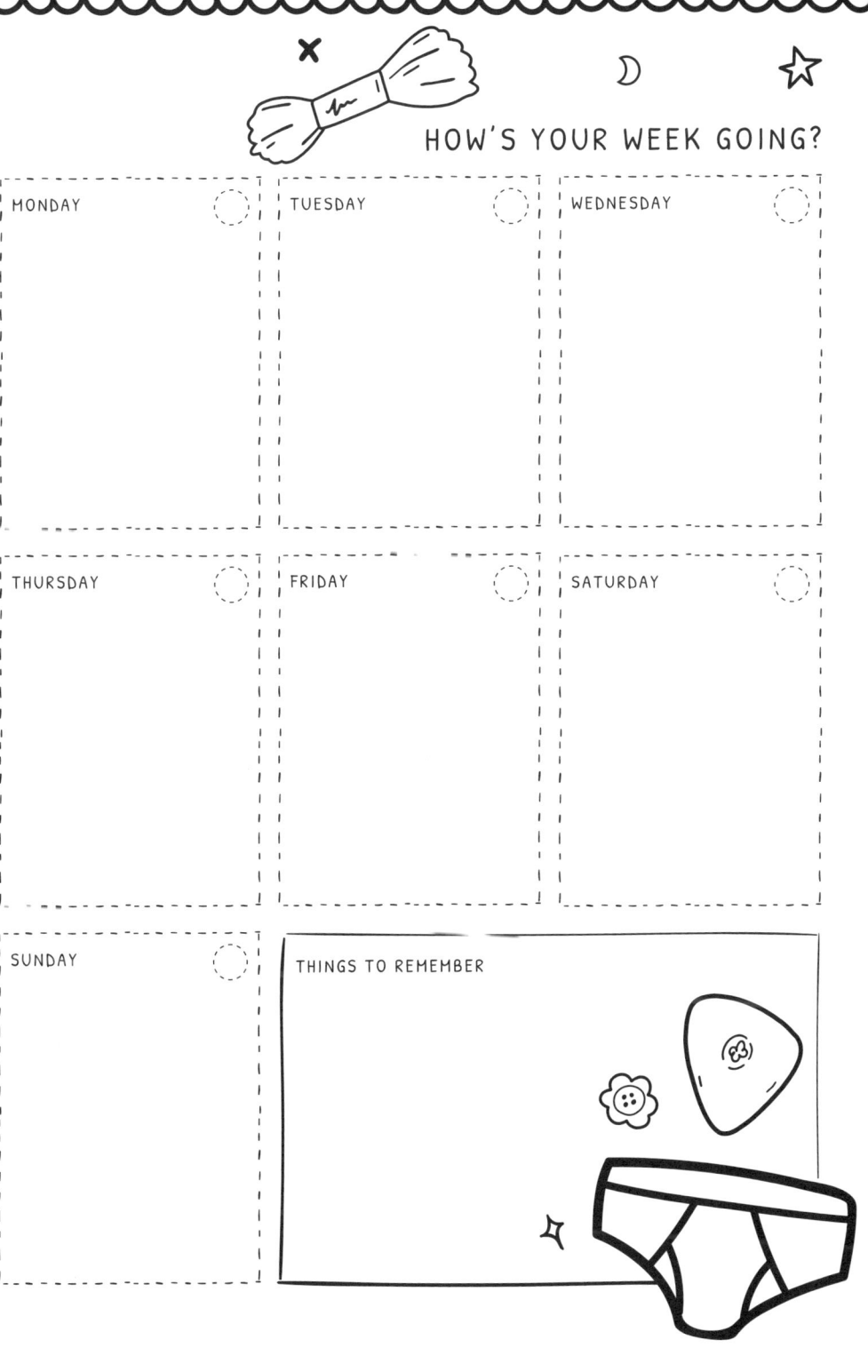

CHAPTER TEN

MONDAY	TUESDAY	WEDNESDAY

THURSDAY	FRIDAY	NOTES

SATURDAY	SUNDAY	

MONDAY

TUESDAY

WEDNESDAY

THURSDAY

FRIDAY

SATURDAY

SUNDAY

TIP EARLY TO BED

To combat the tiredness, it helps to go to bed an hour earlier when you're on your period, or at least get your full 8 hours. Your body is doing a lot of work whilst menstruating so it helps to give yourself some extra rest.

CHAPTER TEN

MONDAY	TUESDAY	WEDNESDAY

THURSDAY	FRIDAY	NOTES

SATURDAY	SUNDAY	

TO DO

○
- -

○
- -

○
- -

○
- -

○
- -

○
- -

○
- -

○
- -

○
- -

○
- -

○
- -

○
- -

○
- -

○
- -

'I can't think of any better representation of
beauty than someone who is unafraid to be herself.'

— EMMA STONE

GOOD vibes only

TIP CHOOSE THE RIGHT UNDERWEAR

Dark colours work best than white or lighter shades when it comes to dealing with potential stains and above all make sure you're comfortable!

'Buy some very big underwear, M&S cotton briefs are my favourite. Within a few months, you will prefer them to your other pants and enter the cult of the granny pants for life.'

– SCARLETT CURTIS

CHAPTER eleven

The first person I talked to about my period wasn't actually a person at all - it was our Jack Russell Terrier, Millie! I'd been suffering from a mysterious tummy ache all day and had decided to take the dogs out to get some fresh air and try to walk it off. Just before I left, I popped to the loo and discovered the little tell-tale stain in my knickers. My mum had been brilliant at explaining about periods to my sisters and me when we were young so it wasn't scary, but I still needed time to process it, so I spent half an hour with my dog, practising how I was going to announce my news when I got home! I don't know what I was worried about, my mum gave me a big hug and we had a cup of tea to celebrate.

MATILDA STANLEY
FREELANCE STYLIST,
FASHION & BEAUTY WRITER

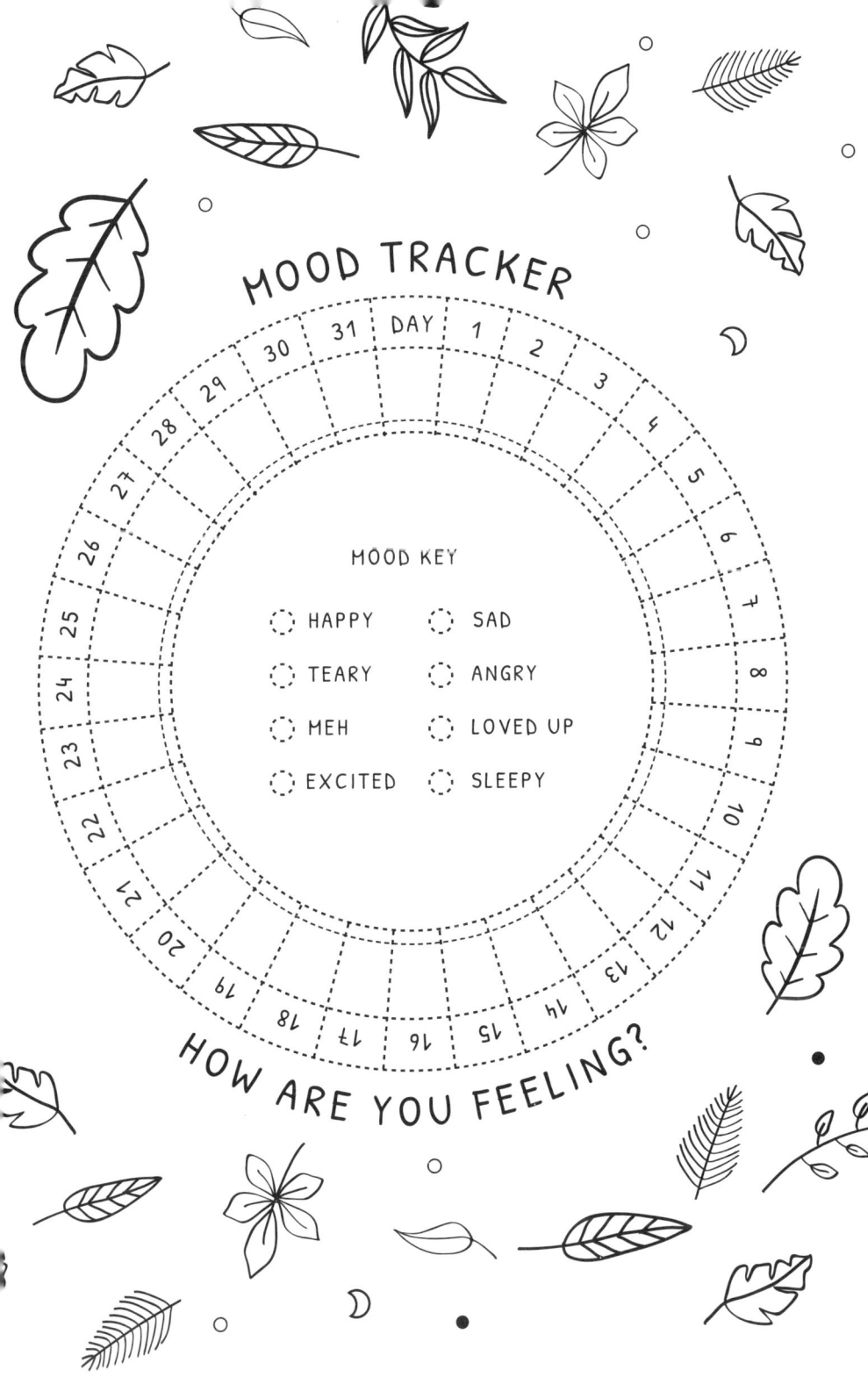

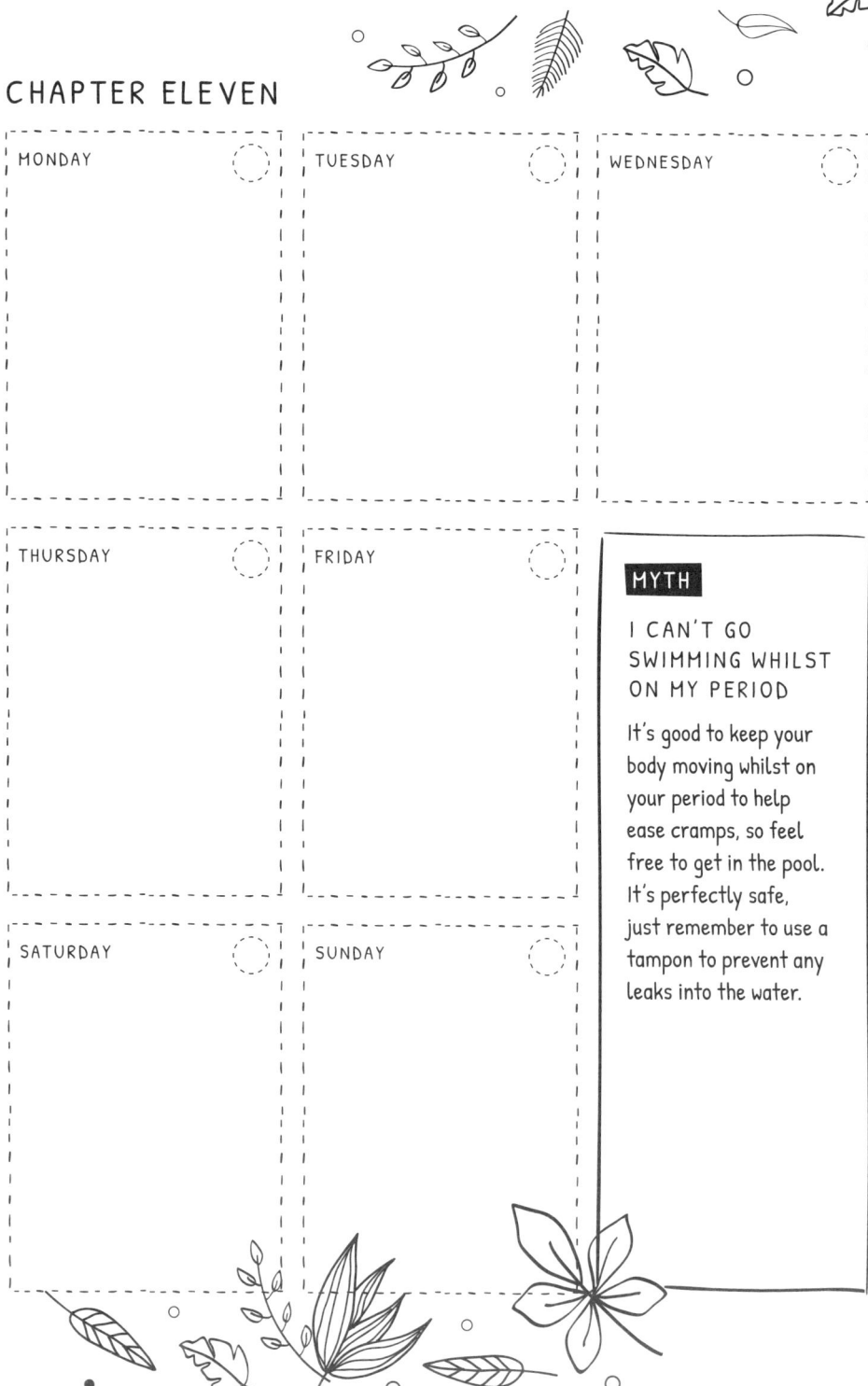

MONDAY

TUESDAY

WEDNESDAY

THURSDAY

FRIDAY

MYTH

I CAN'T GO
SWIMMING WHILST
ON MY PERIOD

It's good to keep your
body moving whilst on
your period to help
ease cramps, so feel
free to get in the pool.
It's perfectly safe,
just remember to use a
tampon to prevent any
leaks into the water.

SATURDAY

SUNDAY

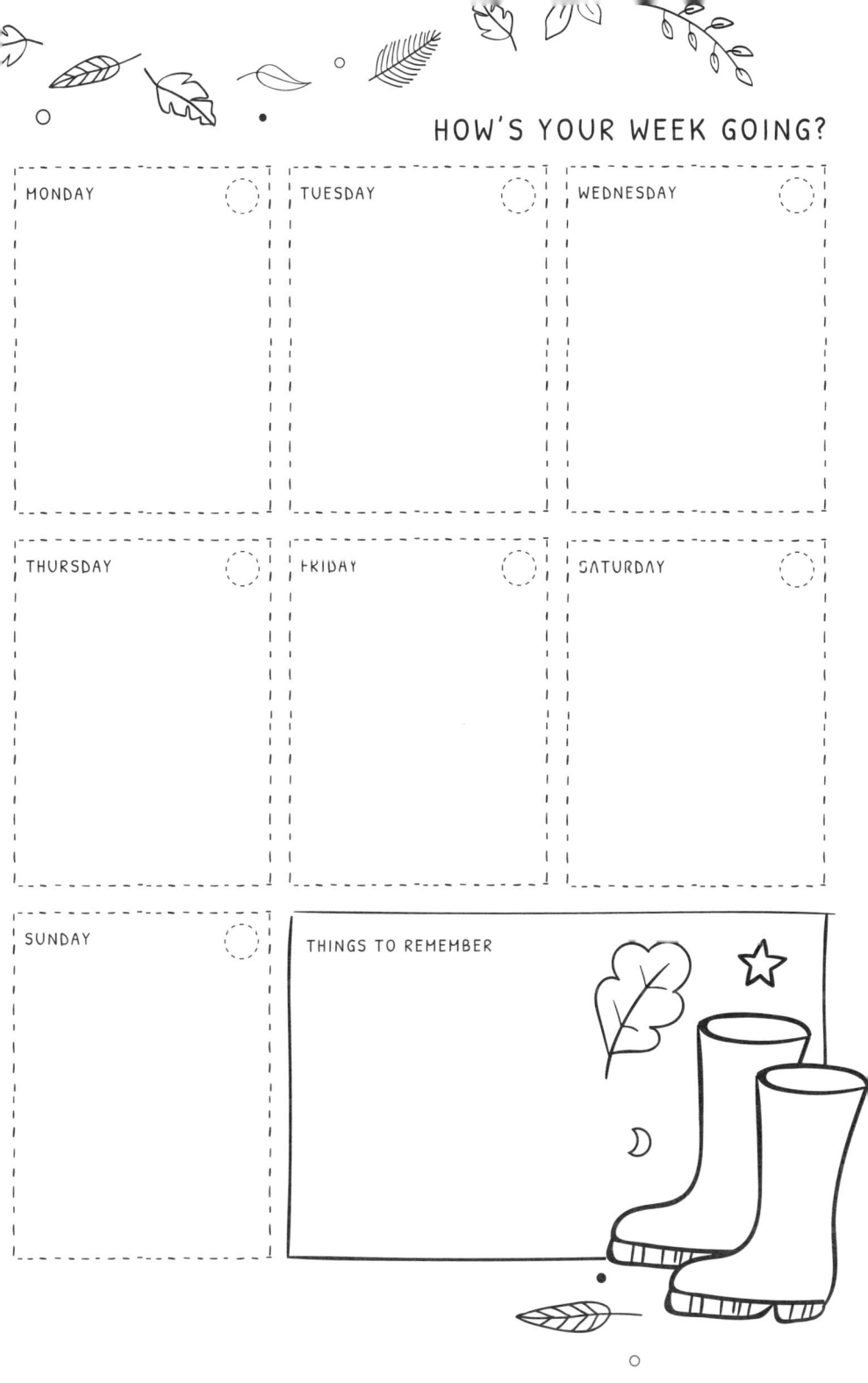

HOW'S YOUR WEEK GOING?

MONDAY

TUESDAY

WEDNESDAY

THURSDAY

FRIDAY

SATURDAY

SUNDAY

THINGS TO REMEMBER

CHAPTER ELEVEN

MONDAY

TUESDAY

WEDNESDAY

THURSDAY

FRIDAY

NOTES

SATURDAY

SUNDAY

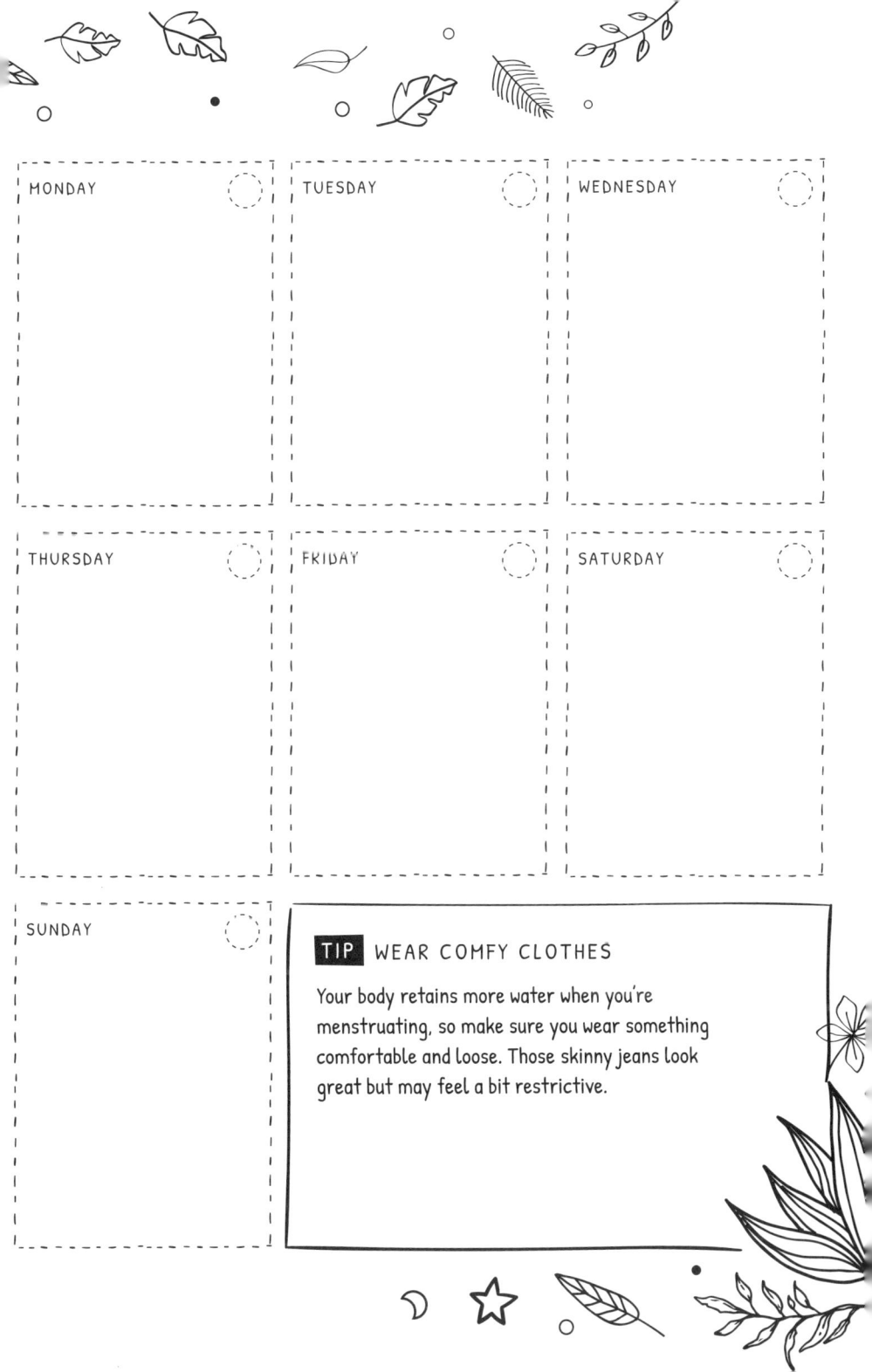

MONDAY

TUESDAY

WEDNESDAY

THURSDAY

FRIDAY

SATURDAY

SUNDAY

TIP WEAR COMFY CLOTHES

Your body retains more water when you're menstruating, so make sure you wear something comfortable and loose. Those skinny jeans look great but may feel a bit restrictive.

CHAPTER ELEVEN

MONDAY

TUESDAY

WEDNESDAY

THURSDAY

FRIDAY

NOTES

SATURDAY

SUNDAY

TO DO

- ○ -------------------------------------
- ○ -------------------------------------
- ○ -------------------------------------
- ○ -------------------------------------
- ○ -------------------------------------
- ○ -------------------------------------
- ○ -------------------------------------

- ○ -------------------------------------
- ○ -------------------------------------
- ○ -------------------------------------
- ○ -------------------------------------
- ○ -------------------------------------
- ○ -------------------------------------
- ○ -------------------------------------

'If you are always trying to be normal,
you'll never know how amazing you can be.'

— MAYA ANGELO

CHAPTER *twelve*

My Mum had given me some pads (this was the 1980s!) in case I had my period. I was mortified as we didn't really talk about stuff like that, but I was grateful I had them as my mates had started talking about getting them. I was eleven, and in LA where I grew up, the early summer sun was shining. One Sunday, we drove out to Lake Elsinore to visit friends of my Dad's from work - me, Mum, Dad and my two annoying little brothers. I was wearing - wait for it! - white shorts and a white t-shirt, with fluorescent leg-warmers (did I mention this was the 80s?). We went out for a walk with this couple of friends of Dad's who I hardly knew, and who didn't have any kids. I had a stomach ache, but it was really low down. When we got back to the house I felt a bit out of sorts and went to the loo - there was a bright red stain all over my pants and (white) shorts. I didn't have the pads but after agonising over it, I took my mum to one side and got her to find some from the woman in the house. In my head, even though I wrapped my jumper around my waist for the rest of the day I was sure the stain was obvious, but nobody else mentioned it. I know this because my little brothers would have thought it hilarious.

JULIE MCKEEN
CEO, SARKA LONDON

MOOD TRACKER

DAY · 1 · 2 · 3 · 4 · 5 · 6 · 7 · 8 · 9 · 10 · 11 · 12 · 13 · 14 · 15 · 16 · 17 · 18 · 19 · 20 · 21 · 22 · 23 · 24 · 25 · 26 · 27 · 28 · 29 · 30 · 31

MOOD KEY

- ○ HAPPY
- ○ TEARY
- ○ MEH
- ○ EXCITED
- ○ SAD
- ○ ANGRY
- ○ LOVED UP
- ○ SLEEPY

HOW ARE YOU FEELING?

CHAPTER TWELVE

MONDAY	TUESDAY	WEDNESDAY

THURSDAY	FRIDAY

MYTH

I CAN'T WASH MY
HAIR WHEN I AM
ON MY PERIOD

There are lots of old
wives tales like 'you
can't wash your hair',
or 'you can't go out in
public' or 'you can only
interact with other
girls/women when on
your period'. The truth
is that you can continue
as normal and do what
you want to. Nothing
has to change with your
normal routine.

SATURDAY	SUNDAY

HOW'S YOUR WEEK GOING?

MONDAY

TUESDAY

WEDNESDAY

THURSDAY

FRIDAY

SATURDAY

SUNDAY

THINGS TO REMEMBER

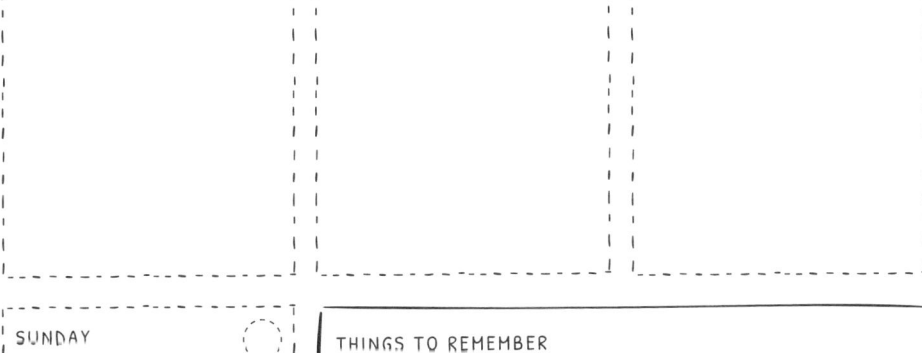

CHAPTER TWELVE

MONDAY	TUESDAY	WEDNESDAY

THURSDAY	FRIDAY	NOTES

SATURDAY	SUNDAY	

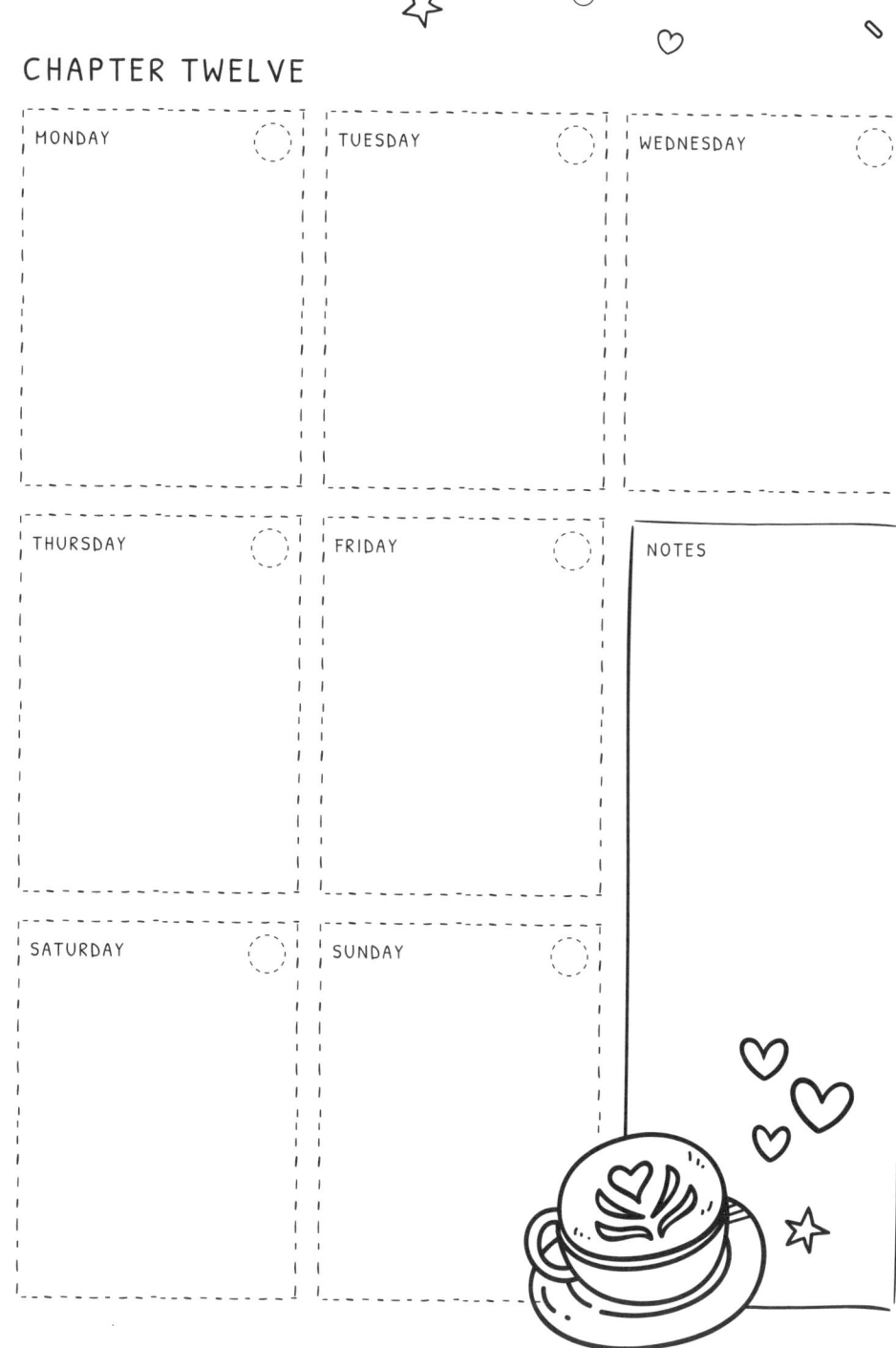

MONDAY	TUESDAY	WEDNESDAY

THURSDAY	FRIDAY	SATURDAY

SUNDAY

TIP IT'S GOOD TO TALK

Talking to your parents about your first period can seem a bit daunting but remember the adult women in your life have been through it before. A good way to approach it is to ask about their experience or if you find it easier to write to them, you can do that too.

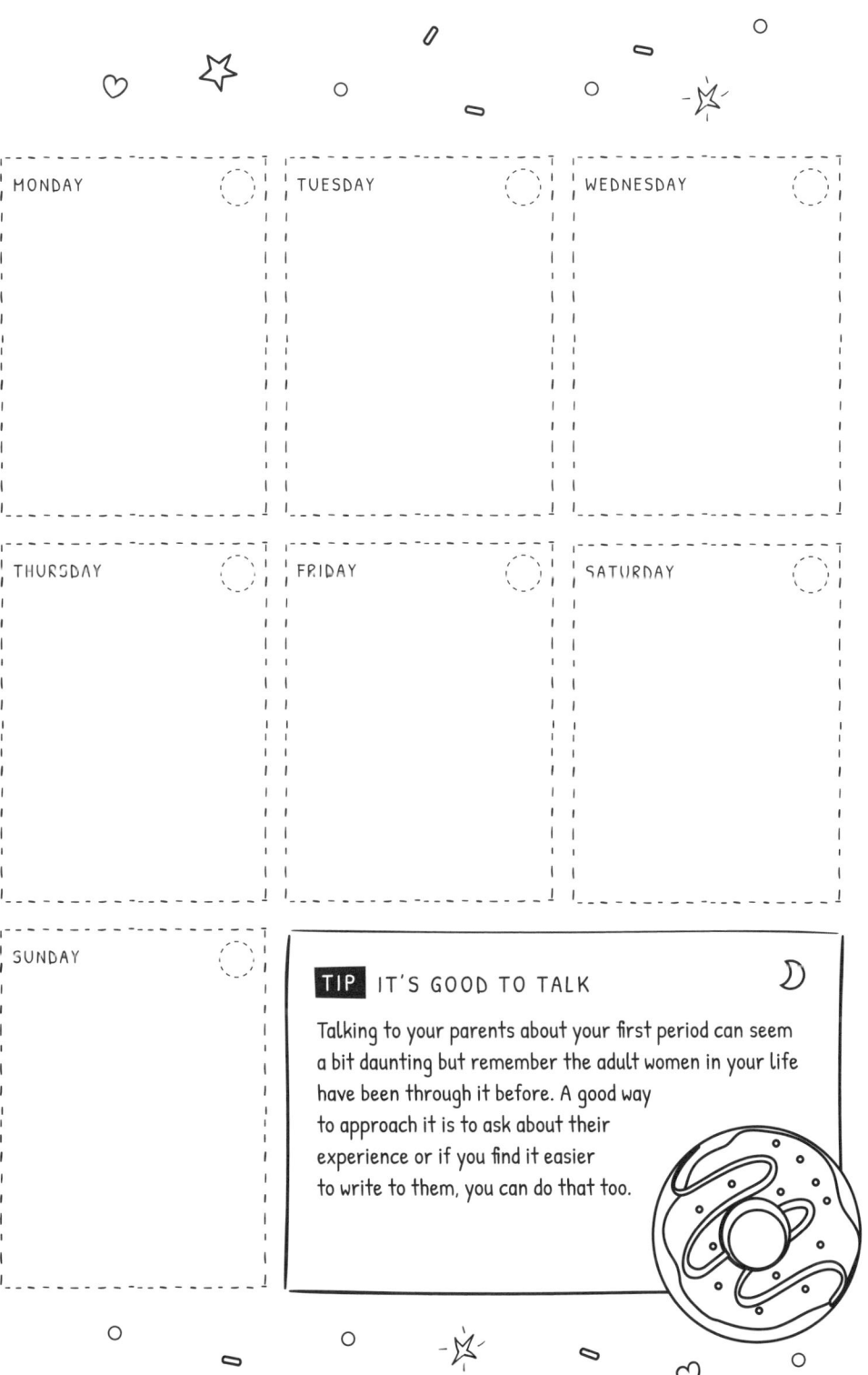

CHAPTER TWELVE

| MONDAY | TUESDAY | WEDNESDAY |

| THURSDAY | FRIDAY | NOTES |

| SATURDAY | SUNDAY |

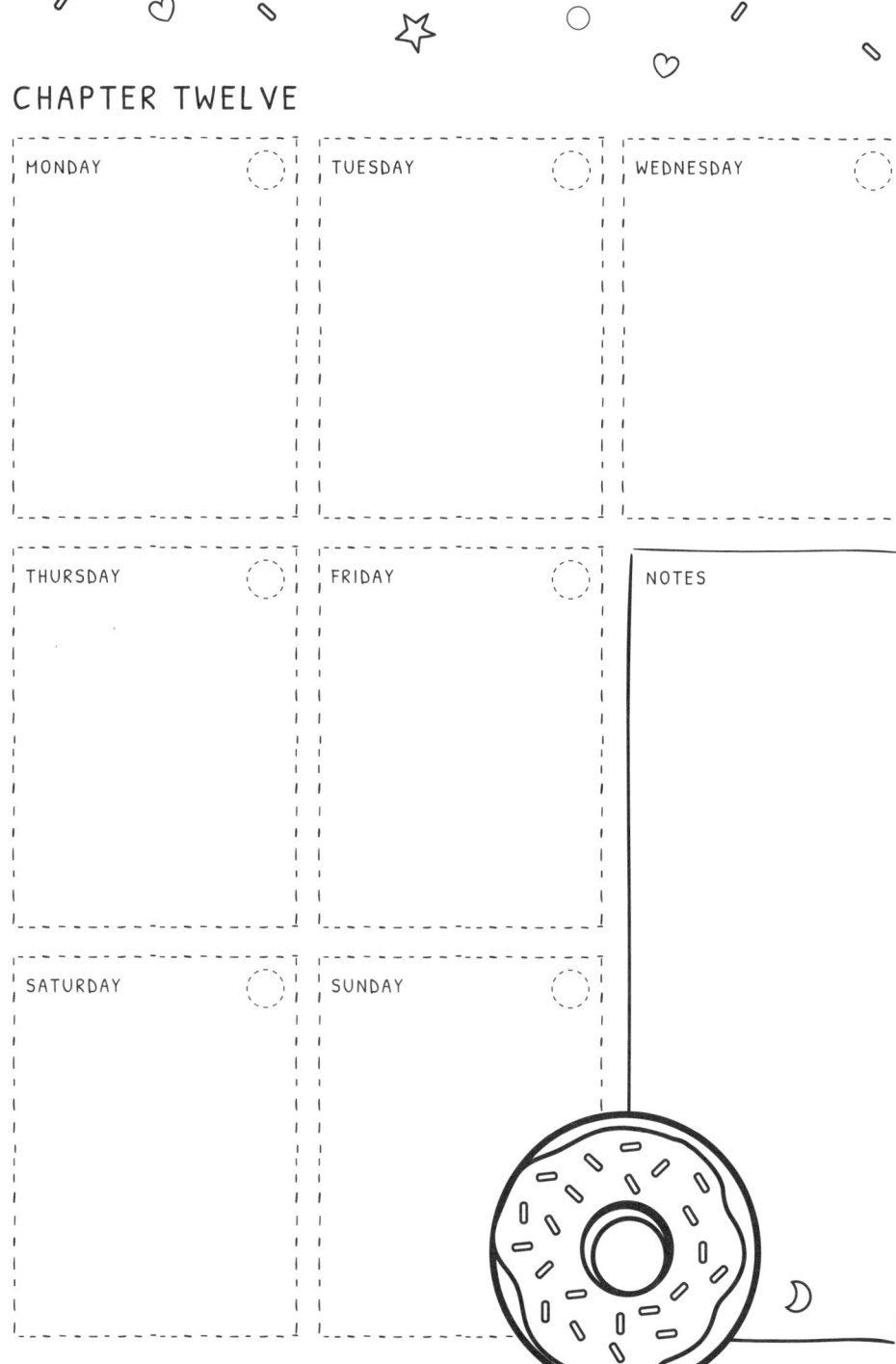

TO DO

- ◌ -------------------------------------
- ◌ -------------------------------------
- ◌ -------------------------------------
- ◌ -------------------------------------
- ◌ -------------------------------------
- ◌ -------------------------------------
- ◌ -------------------------------------

- ◌ -------------------------------------
- ◌ -------------------------------------
- ◌ -------------------------------------
- ◌ -------------------------------------
- ◌ -------------------------------------
- ◌ -------------------------------------
- ◌ -------------------------------------

'Once you figure out what respect tastes like, it tastes better than attention.'

— P!NK

EVERY *girl* HAS A *story*

I remember being at my nan's and needing the toilet before school one random day. I was 11 years old and wondered if I was seeing things in the toilet. Once I realised I wasn't, I screamed for my nan and told her I thought I was dying! She calmed me down and told me we'd have to use tissue temporarily. We soon got some pads, of course. But after that, I remember thinking, 'Wow. Does this mean I'm a grown lady now?'

— LASHANA LYNCH, ACTRESS

NOW IT'S YOUR TURN, WHAT'S YOUR STORY?

GLOSSARY

○ **EGG**

The female reproductive cell made in and released from the ovaries. Also called the ovum.

○ **CERVIX**

This is the opening to the uterus.

○ **FALLOPIAN TUBES**

Tubes through which an egg travels from the ovary to the uterus.

○ **HORMONES**

Natural chemicals made in the body that control the function of cells or organs.

○ **MENSTRUATION/PERIOD**

The monthly shedding of blood and tissue from the uterus that happens when a woman is not pregnant.

○ **OBSTETRICIAN-GYNAECOLOGIST**

A doctor with special training and education in women's health.

○ **OVARIES**

The organs in women that contain the eggs necessary to become pregnant and to make important hormones, such as oestrogen, progesterone and testosterone.

○ **PERIOD CRAMPS**

Cramps can feel like a dull pain in your lower abdomen or lower back. They can be more painful than a dull ache and they'll normally begin 1-2 days before your period arrives.

PREMENSTRUAL SYNDROME
Often called PMS. This is when you experience physical and emotional symptoms, normally a few days before your period starts. Common symptoms include bloating, acne, anxiety, fatigue and food cravings.

PUBERTY
The stage of life when the reproductive organs start to function and a child's body begins to change into an adult's. For women, this is the time when menstrual periods start and the breasts develop.

SEXUAL INTERCOURSE
The act of the penis of the male entering the vagina of the female. Also called 'having sex' or 'making love'.

SPERM
A cell made in the male testes that can fertilise a female egg.

TESTES
The two egg-shaped glands in the scrotum (the sac that hangs under the penis).

TOXIC SHOCK SYNDROME
A rare but life-threatening condition caused by bacteria getting into the body and releasing harmful toxins.

UTERUS
A muscular organ In the female pelvis. During pregnancy this organ holds and nourishes the foetus.

VAGINA
A tube-like structure surrounded by muscles. The vagina leads from the uterus to the outside of the body.

VULVA
The external female genital area.

GIRLH◉OD
THE STORY

Published under licence by Brown Dog Books and
The Self-Publishing Partnership, 7 Green Park Station, Bath BA1 1JB
www.selfpublishingpartnership.co.uk

ISBN printed book: 978-1-83952-232-1
Printed and bound in the UK
This book is printed on FSC certified paper

FSC
www.fsc.org
MIX
Paper from
responsible sources
FSC® C114687